ALIEN
ABDUCTIONS

BF 2050 H68 1999

MAN

GAYLORD F

First published in the UK 1999 by Blandford
A Member of the Orion Publishing Group

Cassell & Co.
Wellington House
125 Strand
London WC2R 0BB

Previously published by Blandford as *The Truth About Alien Abductions*

Distributed in the United States by Sterling Publishing Co., Inc.,
387Park Avenue South, New York, NY 10016-8810

A Cataloguing-in-Publication Data entry for this title is available and may be
obtained from the British Library

ISBN 0-7137-2797-7

Printed in Great Britain by Cox & Wyman Ltd, Reading, Berks.

I'm trying to think of ways to stop it happening. I'm seeing a neuro-psychiatrist soon and maybe he'll diagnose epilepsy or sleep paralysis. Then I can take drugs to prevent it. Perhaps it's an evil spirit like an incubus feeding off my negative thoughts. In which case I'll start going to church. My worst fear is that it's an alien abduction, and then there's absolutely nothing I can do.

LAURA BOND, UFO ABDUCTEE

Acknowledgements

We would like to thank everyone who has allowed us to explore their disquieting and intimate experiences for this book, and pay tribute to those who have played a more practical part: Linda Bidmead, Jennifer Brand, Mark Glover, Alicia Leigh, Juliet Mckinven, Jenny Randles, Jim Singleton, Gary Taylor and the memory of fellow traveller Ken Phillips.

We would also like to thank our publisher and in particular, Commissioning Editor Stuart Booth. Stuart left us in peace to finish the book, long after we had breached the deadline.

PETER HOUGH AND MOYSHE KALMAN

Contents

Introduction 6

1. Magic-carpet Ride 8

2. The Interrupted Journey 19

3. The Tall Ships 27

4. The Green Man 38

5. It Looks like a Demon 55

6. The Devil in our Midst 64

7. It 75

8. The Invasion of Black Brook Farm 91

9. Fields of Dreams 107

10. Before, During and After 114

11. The Phenomenal Intimidators 134

12. Hypnosis and False Memory Syndrome 143

13. Mind Games 155

14. The Sacred Sickness 159

15. Under Examination 172

16. Paralysed 177

17. The Answer to Everything? 182

Bibliography 189

Index 190

Introduction

There cannot be many people in the Western world who are totally unaware of the alien abduction phenomenon. Abductions are one step beyond 'close encounters of the third kind' – the late Professor J. Allen Hynek's definition of a UFO sighting that includes entities. In this next phase of the experience, the witness becomes an unwilling participant in a drama that takes them to the edge of nightmare and beyond.

Apparently, percipients fall victim to beings who take them away for use in bizarre experiments which include painful physical procedures and mind-control techniques. They extract sperm and ova for use in hybrid breeding programmes and show them the destruction of the Earth. Often, the details are locked away in the unconscious, the only clue being a huge slice of time for which the abductee cannot account. There the mystery can remain for years, having a subtle but devastating effect on the victim's life. Eventually, memories leach into the conscious mind in flashbacks, dreams and through the use of hypnotic regression.

Are alien abductions subjective or objective, internal fantasies or hard, cold fact? Is there any independent proof of their objective reality? What is the link between abductions and paranormal experiences? Are extraterrestrials visiting the Earth, or are they visitors from a place much closer to home? How reliable are the explanations put forth by sceptics? What kind of people have these encounters?

This book is the result of a unique collaboration. The authors come from two completely different cultural and professional backgrounds. Peter Hough is a professional writer and investigator of unexplained phenomena, who has been actively interested in UFO-related experiences since 1975. Moyshe Kalman was trained in traditional psychotherapeutic techniques at Boston University and Boston State Hospital, Massachusetts, before settling in Britain.

About five years ago a mutual acquaintance asked Moyshe Kalman if he would like to assist Peter in his investigation of abductees. Moyshe agreed and what followed was an intense programme of enquiry into the claims, beliefs, lives and hidden memories of a number of people, many of which have found their way into this book. At their request we have changed their names to ensure anonymity.

In the following pages we present the results of our research into this highly complex phenomenon. The social standing of many of our interviewees is high. They are the sort of people whom we would trust in almost every other aspect of their personal and professional lives. Their stories will astound any fair-minded person. *We should listen to them very carefully.*

In our search for the truth, we examine the neurological and psychological mechanisms that some claim are responsible for abduction and close-encounter experiences. We tackle the criticism of hypnosis as a tool for memory retrieval and describe the ten-year ordeal of one desperate young woman whom 11 neurologists tried to prove was suffering from a focused form of epilepsy.

Abduction claims are on the increase. The more the subject is aired, the more cases emerge. Is the high public profile of abductions encouraging a greater number of people to fantasize, or is it giving more victims the confidence to come forward?

In truth, no *independent* observer has reported witnessing an abduction. Equally, no one has described coming across a person in a field, or a family parked in a car, in a zombie-like state while hallucinating an abduction experience for an hour or two.

We believe that the growing abduction phenomenon is one of the greatest mysteries to confront humanity. This, the first scientific examination of a number of new cases, will attempt to find the answers to the questions surrounding the phenomenon.

PETER HOUGH AND MOYSHE KALMAN

Chapter 1

Magic-carpet Ride

Dr Simon Taylor, who is currently lecturing in Middle Eastern studies at a British university, told the following story about an incident that took place in Iran in the 1970s. It also involved Dr Taylor's Iranian friend Reza, a distinguished civil servant working with a development organization in the city of Qazuim, west of Tehran.

There were times, especially during the immediate aftermath of Ahar, when I seriously thought that the incident was a sign of madness, or a precursor to it, despite the fact that at the time I had living proof – Reza – that something had actually happened.

From December 1974 until December 1976, I lived and worked in the Iranian capital, Tehran. I was working as an English-language instructor for the then Imperial Iranian Air Force.

Tehran is not the most beautiful of cities. I have often heard it described as the 'arsehole of Asia'. It is only the majestic backdrop of the Elburz Mountains, against which the city leans, that makes life in the capital bearable. It was to the mountains that I went whenever opportunity arose, to escape the oppressive summer heat and the chronic pollution that hangs in a permanent cloud over the city. Mountain walks along the foothills of the Elburz and picnics in the picturesque villages that dot the range are the only real consolation for one who lives in a city built for 2 million people but which houses more than twice that number.

On Thursday afternoon, 16 September 1976, an Iranian friend [Reza] and I set off in his car for the village of Ahar, to the north-east of Tehran. We arrived at around six in the evening and decided to start walking and spend the night in one of the many climbers' cabins that litter the mountainside. After a climb of about an hour we reached one such haven and decided that we had done enough for one day.

The cabin was near a shrine, an imamzadeh, the burial place of one of Prophet Muhammad's descendants. Since this was a popular place of pilgrimage we were surprised to find only a handful of people in and around the cabin.

After hot tea and a light meal we settled down for a game of cards which must have lasted at least a couple of hours. More tea followed, plus several trips to the primitive loo at the back of the cabin. Then we decided to have an early night. Our plan was to rise early, make our way to the next stopping-post, have breakfast and then return to Ahar. We would spend most of Friday in Ahar and return to Tehran in the evening.

By the time we unpacked our sleeping-bags there were only four of us in the cabin: Reza, myself and a father and son. They were on their way back down to the village, but had decided to spend the night on the mountainside. My friend lit the paraffin lamp and we all settled down for the night.

I cannot recall the exact time I woke up. All I know is that the room had become cloyingly warm, the air so sticky and nauseating that I had begun to sweat and then gasp for air as though there was little or no oxygen in the room. My friend was also awake. He must have suspected the lamp, because he was tampering with it in the middle of the room, all the time coughing and wheezing. There was no sign of the father or son, nor their belongings.

Outside I could hear movements around the cabin, as though branches were being snapped, or burning wood crackling. Maybe, I thought, the choking atmosphere was due to a fire in the surrounding trees. Before I could articulate these thoughts, the cabin was rocked by a series of heavy, pounding thumps, as though a demolition crew was trying to bring the hut down on us.

I have never moved so fast in my life. Within seconds we were outside, clad only in T-shirts and long johns, standing in terror and anticipation. I don't know what we expected, but what we saw did not fit in with the thunderous sounds that had forced us out into the dark.

A few feet away stood three men. They were dressed from head to toe in black, rather like the SAS. Each carried a torch-like instrument, and the only feature that I can remember is their eyes: slightly Mongoloid, similar to those of the Turkomen in North-East Iran. But these eyes were much bigger and more lustrous. It was as though the upper part of their faces was all eyes.

Reza opened his mouth to say something, then closed it, seemingly in indecision. I had heard of the SAUAK – the Shah's secret police – and wondered if my friend was on their black list. I had suffered a nasty experience with SAUAK, and figured that if he had reason to fear them, this was a prime opportunity to whisk him away, as they did with countless others who had disappeared.

But they were not from SAUAK. This became clear when they started to speak to us. Not once did they open their mouths, nor did we in order to answer them. Indeed their mouths and noses were covered. Not one word was spoken orally during the whole time we were with them. It was as if their words were transferred into my mind, and I 'heard' myself answer just as one can 'hear' one's own thoughts.

They told me not to be afraid, just pack my things and follow them. My friend must have been told the same, because we found ourselves back inside the cabin, carrying out their instructions, never once looking at or speaking to one another. The three men stood motionless in the doorway.

Once dressed, we followed them outside down the twisting path that led back to Ahar. The route is overhung by trees and bushes and the journey would normally be difficult to attempt at night, but the men brightened the path with their torches and we followed in silence.

After walking a few hundred feet, suddenly, inexplicably, we realized we were no longer on the path, but in some sort of room. Instead of stones and twigs, under our feet lay a thick Persian carpet. It was as beautiful as any seen hanging in a bazaar or behind the windows in Ferdowsi Avenue, the carpet centre of Tehran. This sudden transformation elicited not the slightest tremor of surprise from us. It all 'seemed so right', to use the phrase my friend uttered long after the incident was over.

The men switched off their torches and as soon as they did so the whole place was bathed in the softest of lights. We were in the middle of what seemed to be an oval-shaped room, and were invited to sit cross-legged on the floor. A 'screen' took up the whole of one long wall. I call it that, yet I felt we could have fallen through. We could see the branches of trees and past them the distant lights of the city.

The room began to shake and shudder and we were told not to be afraid, although this time I did feel nervous. The lights of Tehran began to recede and then swung back into view directly beneath us. I gripped the thick carpet, afraid I might fall out. The room was swaying like a cable-car on its way up a mountain. There was a tremendous pressure in my ears and I must have looked alarmed, because one of the men tried to reassure me.

I cannot remember all of the places we 'visited', but I distinctly remember fantastic aerial panoramas of London, New York, Paris and my home city of Birmingham. We saw deserts and frozen wastes of ice and snow, seas – more water than I had ever seen in my life! The pictures were crystal clear and three-dimensional. When we flew near some sheep on an Albanian hillside they were so close I felt I could reach out and touch them. All through the journey the beings were talking to us about the places we were visiting, the people, their habits and beliefs.

Afterwards we were abruptly asked to leave. This we did as orderly and as unquestioningly as when we first arrived. The moment we stepped outside that room it seemed that most of what had happened was already forgotten. We simply got up and walked.

Instead of plush Persian carpet there were now stones and twigs beneath our feet again. The sun was already quite high in the sky and we saw that we were on the approach road to Ahar, no more than a couple of hundred yards from where we had parked the car. Other walkers were coming down from the mountain and my watch read exactly 2 pm. I guessed we had been in the 'room' for five or six hours!

We made our way silently to the car, neither of us daring to say anything. This silence lasted for at least another hour. Then hunger overtook me and I asked Reza to pull over so we could buy kebabs from a roadside stall. We ate our fill and carried on back to Tehran.

A mundane act like eating sheep's-liver kebab seemed to break *the spell. We gushed excitedly about the event we had just experienced and wondered what was behind it. Dreams, hallucinations, brought about by fumes from the paraffin lamp or food poisoning? Hypnosis? Autosuggestion?*

Whichever explanation we evoked, none of them tallied with what seemed to be a very real, physical, tangible experience. Dreams cannot be that real and last for five or six hours. Faulty paraffin lamps, we learned later, are killers. You don't get let off with a few hallucinations! We could not explain what had happened in conventional terms.

The drive back to Tehran was filled with half-baked theories and expressions of amazement. Along the way we were violently sick, but at the time we put it down to the fly-blown liver kebabs.

When they returned to Tehran, the first thing the two men wanted to do was tell someone – anyone – about their experience, but, as Simon put it, 'The grimy streets of Tehran brought us down to earth and made us think of the consequences.'

Simon was engaged to an Iranian girl and realized that the chances of the marriage going ahead would be greatly reduced if his prospective in-laws thought he suffered from hallucinations. Reza, wary of the importance of social acceptance in Iranian society, said they should just forget the whole thing. In fact, he made Simon promise never to tell anyone about the incident.

Within hours of their return to Tehran one of the best-documented UFO incidents on record occurred. Details were released through the American Freedom of Information Act. A report had been sent to the Defense Attaché at the US Embassy who forwarded it to the Defense Intelligence Agency (DIA). An official evaluator described the case as 'outstanding'.

Just after midnight on 19 September 1976 the Imperial Iranian Air Force command post near Tehran received four telephone calls from citizens reporting strange lights moving over the Shemiran area. The assistant deputy commander of operations told them they were probably looking at stars, but after observing one of the objects himself, he decided to scramble an F4 Phantom jet from Shahrokhi Air Force Base to investigate.

As the aircraft approached the brightly lit object, all communications and instrumentation failed. The pilot broke off the intercept and headed back to base. As the F4 turned away from the object, communications and instrumentation returned. A few minutes later a second F4 was launched under the command of a Lieutenant Jafari.

The aircraft acquired a radar lock which showed the object was comparable in size to a Boeing 707 tanker. No shape could be discerned, however, because of its intense brightness. As the fighter closed in, the object began to move away, maintaining its distance. They were travelling south of Tehran when suddenly a small bright object detached itself from the UFO and headed towards the aircraft.

Thinking they were under attack, Jafari attempted to fire an AIM-9 missile, but at that instant the weapons control panel and all communications went dead. The aircraft turned away and the small object returned to its parent craft. Normal power was resumed. As the crew made for base, they saw another small object leave the UFO and land on a dry lake bed. Jafari was so shaken by the close encounter that he had to ask the control tower to guide him back to Shahrokhi Air Base. The lake area was searched later that morning, but nothing was found.

Simon was in the right place to report on these incidents. He said there were many sightings and talk 'about aliens landing in the holy city of Qum, of abductions in Mashhad, and people found wandering in a daze in the middle of the salt lake between Qum and Isfahan'. However, he thought many of these claims should be examined critically. Despite his connections with the Iranian Air Force he was unable to discover any further details.

In December, Simon flew home with his fiancée to England, where they were married. The couple were due to return to Iran in the new year, but the mere idea of going back made Simon ill. The incident had shattered his nerves and may have been responsible for other, long-term physical conditions, including crushing headaches which began immediately after it happened. He told us: 'The first few days back at work were hell. I began to hate my job, and the headaches I was getting regularly made things worse. Whenever I tried to think about what had happened, they returned.' Twenty years on, migraine attacks occur whenever Simon dwells on the experience, or attempts to write about it.

The only thing that kept the young man from madness was the

comforting fact that his friend had been with him that night. However, Reza was becoming elusive, as Simon explained:

He was the only person I could pour my heart out to, but his visits to the capital became less frequent. Before, he had come to Tehran almost every weekend. Between the incident and my departure in December, he had come to see me no more than three times. I told him that we had to get help. I was not sure what kind of help, but a doctor of some kind. He could see how it was affecting me, and I could see what it was doing to him.

Finally Reza refused to discuss the incident at all and suggested that Simon should see a mullah, or Muslim holy man, for comfort. He warned him that if he did so, however, he was to report the experience as if he had been alone at Ahar. Simon was devastated.

'This deprived me of any proof,' he said. 'He was deliberately sweeping it under the carpet, and told me never to talk about it to him again. That was effectively the end of our friendship.'

At that time Simon's fiancée knew nothing of the events on the slopes of the Elburz Mountains, but was aware something was wrong, and worried that Simon might have a brain tumour.

Once in England, he felt as if a great weight had been lifted from his shoulders and the headaches temporarily disappeared. Although it meant giving up their lucrative employment in Iran, Simon persuaded his wife that they should stay in England and further their academic studies. He busied himself in a vain attempt to bury all memory of Ahar.

Around 1977 Simon developed gynaecomastia, an embarrassing swelling of the breasts. This became so pronounced that in June 1981 he was forced to undergo plastic surgery. Further medical problems were to follow: in July 1986 Simon suffered what he thought was a heart attack (it was pericarditis, an inflammation of the sac around the heart) and in 1990 he began a year of malaise and fatigue which was eventually diagnosed as post-viral syndrome – myalgic encephalomyelitis, or ME:

At first it felt as though I had a severe bout of flu which got worse. The flu-like symptoms eased off to be replaced by excruciating muscle pains and overwhelming fatigue. Plus loss of short term memory, inability to concentrate, aversion to bright lights and loud sounds, unpredictable mood swings and great black stretches of depression.

My health problems may turn out to be another legacy of Ahar. I cannot directly attribute them to our experience there, but I do vaguely recollect being touched around the chest region by one of the entities.

The couple returned to Iran in January 1978 to earn money to pay for their education in England. Although they did not realize it, the revolution which was to depose the Shah was just around the corner. During this time Simon saw Reza twice. The Iranian agreed to meet him providing Ahar was not mentioned. Simon and his wife came back to England in February 1979.

From then until 1986 Simon heard nothing from Reza except for greetings cards he received marking the Iranian New Year. Simon's letters remained unanswered and his attempts to speak to Reza on the telephone came to nothing. Then, in January 1988, he received a bizarre message. The telephone rang, and a voice said: 'Reza has joined Reza.' More intrigued than alarmed, he tried Reza's office number, introducing himself as 'a close friend'. Reza, he was told, had died a year ago, almost to the day, of cancer of the liver.

Simon wrote to Reza's brother in Erzerum in eastern Turkey to express his condolences, and in return received a photograph of his friend, taken a year before his death. Simon told us: 'It is now the only photograph I have of Reza.' With the picture was a letter describing the strange circumstances of his demise.

In the immediate aftermath of Ahar, Reza had confided in Simon that he knew when, where and how he would die, although he would not elaborate further. Now Simon discovered that Reza had also told his family. This, his brother said, had come as more of a shock to them than his eventual death.

A few days before his death, Reza discharged himself from hospital and travelled hundreds of miles to Mashhad, a town in eastern Iran, on the border with Russia. There he checked into a small guest-house near a shrine dedicated to the Imam Reza, a descendant of the prophets. Reza had indeed joined with Reza.

On the evening before his body was discovered, a man answering his description was seen in the central courtyard of the shrine with a large black bag bursting with fresh ten-*tuman* banknotes. These he freely distributed to passers-by. Reza's body was found by a maid the following morning in his room. Simon added:

There was nothing to suggest suicide. No note, no pill bottles, no rope and no gun. Since an autopsy was not performed – it is forbidden in Islamic law – the truth remains a matter of conjecture. He was buried in Mashhad the following day.

Deprived of being with him in his last months, and at his death, I still mourn my friend. The last letter I received from him was in broken English – he had just started classes – and his attempts at the new language were childlike and touching. He also enclosed a passport-sized photograph of himself, which I immediately fixed in one of our albums. That photograph is no longer there. I do not remember removing it, and I have no reason to suspect anyone else. I have searched everywhere. I often doubt ever having received such a thing, although I know I did.

Simon's research led him to believe that Reza had been pivotal to the experience at Ahar.

I think that the idea of crisis and personal trauma as a 'trigger' for Ahar-type experiences should be given more careful consideration. Reza was the first real friend I had in Iran. He introduced me to its language, culture and history. I'll always be grateful to him for turning a potentially disastrous time into a tolerable and even enjoyable one. But it didn't take me very long to realize that his aspirations went considerably further than the purely platonic.

Simon made it clear he was not interested, and Reza never pushed his homosexuality, saying that he valued their friendship above everything else.

On 31 August 1976 my girlfriend and I became engaged. I can appreciate now what this must have meant for Reza. No more trips to Isfahan or the Caspian Sea, no more picnics on the slopes of Damavand, no more nights of wine and poetry – all the things we had shared and enjoyed so much. And of course the death of hope for the one thing we (thankfully) hadn't shared. Even if the events of 16 September had not happened, that weekend would probably have been the last I spent with him anyway. To some extent I feel he sensed this.

On the evening of his arrival from Qazvin – he came to Tehran every Wednesday and stayed over until Saturday – he seemed inexplicably distant and on edge, although on the following day, as we drove to Ahar, he was his old cheerful self, full of plans to learn English properly and visit relatives in Turkey. In retrospect he seemed almost too cheerful, as if he was putting on a front for my benefit.

I don't believe that what happened to us was purely psychological, although much of it – the 'craft' and the amazing 'flight' around the world – most probably was. The entities, whatever their true identity, were real. Of this I have no doubt. They could touch and be touched, see and be seen, 'speak' and be spoken to. At Ahar we were not dreaming.

There are many aspects of the incident that have remained hidden. I know they are there, on what I call the 'tip of my memory'. They move around ghost-like at the back of my mind. I know they are there, but not what they are. It is like something seen from the corner of one eye. You look around; there's nothing. But you know there was something, and that now it's hiding. Heavily veiled memories of Ahar plague me, things that happened, things that were done and said, memories that reach the point of revealing themselves, of disrobing, only to scurry back into the shadows.

I know that many of the dreams I have had since are reflections, if not actual replays of that night. But I wake up never remembering. There is music, the most beautiful music I have ever heard, which runs like a leitmotif through the dreams. One morning I could hear the music in my dream. I made a conscious effort to memorize the tune. I must have been humming and la-la-ing out loud because it woke my wife.

More recently I had what must be the first substantial dream of Reza since I heard of his death. In the dream he was reading poetry – he was a great lover of classical Persian poetry – and he was reciting one of Mowlavi's. He was also talking about 'that night'. The poem was Mowlavi's 'From an unborn child in the womb', which is an allegory on resurrection and the hereafter. I feel he was trying to tell me he was forewarned of his own death. I had sensed this during the 'abduction' and the dream seemed to confirm it.

I then had what I believe is called a 'false awakening'. Turning my head on the pillow, I saw Reza lying next to me. Quite unfazed, I reached across to touch him, at which point I woke up and he was gone.

I now wonder if the dream was intended as a warning. Several days later a routine blood test revealed abnormal liver function. Thankfully it is believed to be the result of the drugs I am taking, and is thus, hopefully, a transient condition.

Dr Simon Taylor has spent the intervening years searching for an answer to the experience. He now believes he understands the nature of the forces behind his, and Reza's, abduction. These are discussed in a later chapter.

Chapter 2

The Interrupted Journey

Rain smacked the tarmacked surface of the car park like tracer fire. Samantha bundled her daughter Lizzie into the car, then rushed around to the back and helped Malcolm unload the groceries. As she returned the empty trolley and retrieved her ten-franc deposit, the irony of the situation was not lost on her. They had taken their Easter break in the South of France to escape the Manchester weather, but the rain seemed to have followed them from England. Now, thankfully, they were homeward bound. It was the evening of 29 April 1995.

The supermarket was on the outskirts of Annecy, at Epagny. As their parking ticket verified, they had arrived at 5.27 pm. They were hoping to have a meal and refuel, as their petrol tank was down to about a quarter, but the pumps were closed. Ahead of them lay a two-hour drive to Dijon, where they intended to stay at a hotel for the night and set off early in the morning for Calais and the hover-craft back to England.

After the family had eaten, they went into the supermarket and bought wine and chocolates to take home. Their grocery bill is timed at 7.50 pm. They left a few minutes later, assuming they would find another service station before long. There was a 25 km (16 mile) journey to the autoroute that would take them to Dijon, a total distance of around 250 km (160 miles).

The wipers slopped across the windscreen as dusk closed in, aggravating the poor driving conditions. Samantha became concerned for her husband:

Malcolm was at the wheel. Lizzie was asleep on the back seat. He kept saying, 'I can't see.' It was terrifying. In the end I said, 'Look, will you stop?' I was very tired, but I said I would drive until we reached the autoroute.

Malcolm later told Peter Hough that the headlights of the oncoming cars dazzled him severely, because he wears contact lenses.

They pulled over in the small town of Frangy, and quickly changed places. Malcolm complained he was extremely tired and dozed off. He woke up just before they reached the tollbooth for the A40.

The autoroute took them up over the Alps, across a huge viaduct, and wound through tunnels cut into the mountainous landscape. Fog swallowed the car and Samantha was swamped with guilt. It had been her idea to take this route; she wanted to visit Annecy so that she could describe it to her mother, who was considering a trip to France. She remembers thinking:

Why did I choose this route? What's wrong with me? We're not going to find a hotel, and it's all my fault! I was feeling really dreadful. Malcolm didn't say anything, but I was musing: 'He must think I'm really stupid, bringing us up into the mountains.'

It was very foggy, so I wasn't doing, like 90 miles an hour. But I was still travelling quite fast, about 60 or so. I remember coming down the mountainside and thinking, 'We've got to swap seats and find some petrol'. Somewhere between 11.30 and 11.45 pm we pulled into a service station.

The service station was at Caignes Cordon, 65 km (40 miles) from Epagny. By this time the rain had stopped and the fog had disappeared. They left a few minutes later, aware that something was not quite right, but too tired to wonder what it was. They skirted around Bourg en Bresse towards Macon and the A6 north. Malcolm was driving now. The autoroute became strangely deserted. Suddenly they were not alone. Malcolm screwed up his eyes at something ahead, to their left.

'What are those lights?' he asked.

Samantha looked up.

As Malcolm told Peter Hough:

At first I thought, It's a helicopter, then I looked and couldn't imagine why a helicopter would have eight beams of light. It didn't make sense. We opened the sun-roof to listen for the rotor blades. There was nothing. It wasn't a helicopter – we knew it wasn't a helicopter. Then I thought it was a train. I kept looking to see if I could see railway lines, but I couldn't. We had seen trains earlier.

There was something very unusual about the lights (see plate section), as Malcolm explained:

They were all equal lengths – they didn't shine on anything. They stopped in mid-air. The beams were clearly defined and just stopped abruptly. As we watched, they spun, twisted and swivelled, as if they were attached to something.

The 'something' dropped behind and vanished when traffic appeared. Once the road was deserted again the lights returned, this time on the other side of the autoroute. It happened a number of times. Malcolm decided to test the train hypothesis:

I realized that a train would keep at a fairly constant speed, so I slowed down to 40. I expected it to go whizzing past, but it remained the same distance behind us, even when I speeded up to 110. Then it would drop back, and draw closer, the lights spinning and twisting.

The object was 90 metres (100 yd) away at its closest. Still desperate to rationalize the phenomenon, Malcolm and Samantha wondered if the lights were from cars on a parallel road, but the maneouvrability of the object ruled that out. They had to eliminate all the conventional explanations. Samantha said:

The only thing I've seen which mirrors the movement of that thing was a scene from Star Wars. *There's a part where a small fighter spacecraft comes down close to the surface of a planet, and has to weave from side to side to avoid enemy fire. Then I thought, 'Perhaps it is a UFO. That's what Malcolm thinks too, and that's why he's behaving so strangely.' I said, 'Do you think it's a spaceship or something?' I know what led me to think that. Earlier in the day we had driven through some very spectacular scenery, and there were some formations like that huge rock in* Close Encounters.

As the thought took hold, the couple grew desperate for the company and reassurance of other vehicles. Samantha described what was happening:

I got panicky, and said to Malcolm that we must keep up with the other cars. Whenever we dropped back or overtook, and were on our own again, the lights appeared next to us. When we were with other cars it disappeared.

Up ahead on the inside lane appeared two lorries carrying British company names. Malcolm sandwiched the car between the two giants. This was out of character: on motorways, Malcolm usually keeps to the outside lane, driving at high speed. If anything happened, he planned to signal for the truck drivers to stop and explain what was going on.

After a few kilometres some of Malcolm's confidence returned and he wanted to pull over and look more closely at the lights, but his wife was concerned for Lizzie's safety, so they carried on. In the hour since leaving the service station they had covered a long distance, but for some reason they were greatly behind schedule.

Kilometre after kilometre came and went, but they could not find anywhere to stay and pushed on past Dijon. At around 2 am they arrived at the Chateauvillain Orges service station near Chaumont, a distance of 275 km (170 miles) from Caignes Cordon, and spent a good hour making sure the strange lights were not around. They felt safe surrounded by other people and decided to spend the remainder of the night sleeping in the car. Malcolm stretched across the front seats. Samantha wrapped little Lizzie in a duvet and placed her on the parcel shelf, then settled herself on the back seat.

'We didn't sleep very well and woke up at six o'clock,' she recalls. 'Then, suddenly, blood started to pour from my nose.'

Samantha was worried, it was highly unusual. 'I've never had a nosebleed before – not a proper one. Occasionally, I've blown my nose and burst a blood vessel, but not like this.'

It felt sore, too. There was a long scratch inside her right nostril.

Samantha found it hard to believe that she could have scratched herself and not remember it. When the bleeding stopped, Samantha took Lizzie to the toilet, where a worse shock awaited her.

'Lizzie was bleeding from the bottom.'

The little girl became hysterical.

Malcolm and Samantha are professional people. He is a company director and she a regional manager for a major British charity. Both were adopted children. They had Lizzie in their early thirties. Lizzie is a bright young thing who, from a very early age, had ambitions to be a ballerina.

Before their encounter, Malcolm and Samantha tended towards scepticism on the subject of UFOs. Could the object they saw have been a helicopter, perhaps a military aircraft, having 'a bit of fun'? Samantha dismissed this possibility:

Since 1980 my work has involved driving thousands of miles, often late at night. I've seen odd lights, but I've never before thought I'd been followed by a UFO. I know at first hand the racket a helicopter makes at close proximity. The autoroute was deserted and quiet; you would hear the noise. There was no helicopter.

In addition to the nosebleed, Samantha has suffered hair loss since the encounter:

My hair has changed. It has become limp and lifeless, and much thinner. I can run my fingers through it, and by the end of the day there's quite an amount of hair. That's not normal for me.

When photographs taken of Samantha on holiday before the encounter are compared with her appearance afterwards, a marked difference in her hair is apparent. Hair loss is often indicative of psychological stress.

It was on the Monday, when they were safely back home, that Malcolm and Samantha's nagging doubts about their journey grew from an itch to an open sore, demanding attention. They consulted road-maps, working out times and mileages. Within a few minutes the truth dawned on them. It had taken three and a half hours to travel the first 65 km (40 miles). That was the distance between the supermarket and the service station at Caignes Cordon.

Had they only covered 65 km (40 miles)? Supposing in the terrible weather conditions they had taken a detour without realizing? Malcolm insists they did not.

'It was only a few miles to the autoroute. There's no other motorway in between to cause confusion. If we had done a detour it would have been blatantly obvious.'

Malcolm, Samantha and Lizzie could not have been driving for three hours. They left the supermarket with little more than a quarter of a tank of fuel – just enough to get them the 65 km (40 miles) to the service station.

'When we filled up, the tank was empty. On average, three hours' driving uses up about three-quarters of a tank. Where were we for two and a half hours?' asks Malcolm.

Malcolm and Samantha independently made some sketches of the incident. They produced near-identical drawings of the lights. Samantha made an additional drawing. It showed a truncated cone, with two matchstick people standing inside.

The second sketch came about after a session of hypnosis carried out by her husband, who is a qualified hypnotherapist. The hypnosis itself was not very productive, but afterwards, Samantha was troubled by strange images:

I had this picture when I shut my eyes. In the picture I was standing inside a large black cone with the top cut off. What I drew was not what I actually saw – that would be impossible to convey. The picture represents how it would look to an observer. The object I was in was not something solid, but the difference between light and dark. It was light and dark. It didn't make sense.

Although Malcolm said nothing at the time, disturbing images had flashed through his mind while they were being tailed:

It was as if someone had made a video film of our journey. I was watching it as if it had happened to another family. They were driving along the road and suddenly the car disappeared into nothing. Suddenly it went quiet, then the car reappeared and they were back on the road again. I felt it was trying to tell me something, that my subconscious was trying to tell me there was a gap.

After they discovered there was a 'missing' period of time, two and a half hours they couldn't account for, Samantha felt that the lights had not been chasing them at all. There was another possibility:

We thought we were going to be abducted, but they were not trying to catch us, they were saying goodbye. I felt they were ensuring we were all right, making sure we were safely on our way. Like you would with someone who was a bit stupid. Or by watching a child home.

Malcolm conjectured: 'I don't think they meant us any real harm. If they can wipe out two and a half hours of memory, they could just as easily wipe us out.'

They thought that was the end of the matter, but, as is common in these cases, this was not to be. Samantha woke up one night, disturbed by a strange dream. In the dream, she was in a room with Malcolm. Before them stood a humanoid creature with large black eyes. What made it worse was that Malcolm could not see the creature.

Then, in the early hours of the morning of Monday, 4 December 1995, Samantha was woken up by the sound of her daughter crying hysterically. It was as if she was screaming at something in her room. Samantha tried to move but found herself paralysed. At that moment the bedroom curtains lit up brightly and there was a whooshing sound from outside.

She shouted at Malcolm, who eventually stirred, and told him to go and see what was wrong with Lizzie. To her amazement, instead of rushing into the child's room, he went over to the window and pulled aside the curtains. 'There's something there,' he muttered. 'Someone's digging up the road.'

Then he went to check on their daughter, and Samantha successfully fought off the paralysis. She climbed out of bed and looked outside. There was something glowing in the road, but she could not make out what it was. She saw a number of men wearing boiler suits digging up the garden. Malcolm returned and said that Lizzie was all right; she had been having a nightmare. They both went back to bed and fell asleep.

The following morning, an examination of the road and garden provided no evidence of the events of the previous night. Malcolm remembered Lizzie crying, and looking through the window, but denied he had seen anything. However, it was alarming to discover that both Samantha and Lizzie were bleeding from their anuses. This was the second time the mother and daughter had bled after a UFO encounter. Peter Hough asked Samantha why she did not take the little girl to see her doctor. She replied:

You must remember that in my job I liaise with social workers. If the bleeding was caused through some sort of injury, my doctor would have no choice but to report the matter to Social Services. That would start an investigation – and no one is going to believe it was connected with UFOs!

As for herself, she would rather remain ignorant. The incident made her realize something. 'I don't know what is really happening, but if they can come and do whatever it is they do, with Malcolm here, then there is no defence against this thing.'

Three or four days after the incident Lizzie came up to her mother and made a curious remark: 'Mummy, tell me what I was dreaming. I can't remember.' Samantha said it was as if Lizzie '. . . partially remembered a dream which included me, and because of that, to her childish way of thinking, she assumed I would know what happened.'

Over Easter 1996, the couple retraced much of their original route across France. The rerun cleared up any remaining doubts they may have had, convincing them that they had not made a mistake: there was a period of missing time they could not explain.

'The whole thing is crazy,' Samantha told Peter Hough. 'How can three people disappear like that, then carry on as if nothing has happened?'

Chapter 3

The Tall Ships

Janet and Harry were a couple when they shared a bizarre experience in August 1992. Today they are still good friends and allowed us to interview them, exploring their memories using hypnosis. Janet is a computer banking executive and Harry is a transatlantic businessman. Amongst his close friends Harry numbers a retired American four-star general who was in charge of tactical air command for the US Air Force.

The day started with a trip to the Albert Docks in Liverpool to witness the Tall Ships Parade. This was the largest gathering of sailing-ships in recent maritime history and the event attracted thousands of people. Janet and Harry jostled with the crowd on the quayside, taking in the amazing sight. Harry commented: 'There was a real carnival atmosphere. It was a normal day with Janet, having arguments half the time and fun the rest.'

They came back to Janet's flat and made tea. Everything seemed quite ordinary. Afterwards they went to bed and the next thing Janet remembers is waking up at 3 am in a state of 'absolute terror'. She told us: 'I wasn't paralysed but I couldn't move my arm to switch on the light just in case something was there.'

When she did eventually switch on the light everything seemed normal – except the way she felt.

'I've woken up from nightmares in the past and the feeling quickly turns to relief upon realizing it was "just a dream". This was no nightmare – of that I am certain.'

She felt that she had been 'somewhere', and then 'landed' back in her bed, 'not thrown but put back'.

I woke up Harry, which is something I never usually do. I said, 'Harry, I don't know how to say this but something's happened, different, changed somehow.' I felt something physical had occurred, like somebody had flicked a switch. He was just staring at me, and asked, 'What is it?' I said I didn't know – but it wasn't a nightmare.

Harry remembered seeing 'something more substantial than a shadow' on the bed when he awoke. He also caught a glimpse of 'two pools of reflection' which disappeared, as if they had gone through a doorway which had then closed up. 'I got an impression of depth as the lights receded,' he told us. Ten minutes later, when the pair had recovered, Janet began to remember what had happened.

She recollected lying down with bright lights all around her. It reminded her of an operating theatre. There were a number of beings she described as 'faceless' around her. Janet feels that her abductors had faces, but her mind blocked them out. She believes that during this stage she was 'given something' to calm her down: 'I didn't go to sleep, I wasn't paralysed, but I couldn't move. I felt heavy. I knew they were doing something and I was indignant.'

The next thing she remembered was being in another room with several other people who were gathered around a strange man:

The funny thing was he had on this odd black fedora-type hat. He was small, very pale and had huge oval eyes that were very dark. When I looked into those eyes I experienced an incredible longing to be there. They seemed to contain the whole universe, and I could have lost myself in them, like being swallowed up by a good painting.

Janet said he was not threatening, but seemed to possess great knowledge. He was passing some of that knowledge on and she had the feeling that similar conversations had taken place before. However, she could not remember much of what was said. He spoke of mankind's origins and how we had been genetically engineered. Our spirit was separate from the body, he confirmed, and they saw nothing wrong in tampering with the physical part of us.

After that she found herself in a long, cold, grey tunnel. There was a man in the tunnel whom she recognized, although she had not seen him since she was 12.

I'd never thought about him; he didn't mean anything to me. Now he was in this tunnel, or corridor, with me. At school he had been very bright, now he seemed deranged. His head was lolling, and saliva trickled from his mouth. I remember one of them saying he had been pushed too far; they hadn't realized he was so weak.

They were taking her into the same room the man had come from. Janet feared that madness awaited her, but despite her remonstrations she was taken inside. There she saw a normal-looking man who seemed to be a medical doctor. He told her, 'We're going to have to alter you because something's not working right.'

'I remember struggling,' Janet told us, 'and the next thing I knew I was back in bed. Despite having difficulty for many years, that night I conceived.'

Janet's conviction that she became pregnant on 15 August is, of course, circumstantial. It is based on the extreme feelings that swept over her that night upon being 'put back' in bed. From then on she was violently ill. Before that she had enjoyed good health.

This was not morning sickness. According to my doctor and the specialists I saw, they could find nothing wrong. I suffered palpitations, cold spots, general pain, sore eyes and indescribable migraines. Hitherto I had only had two a year – now I was getting two a day. I also experienced extreme lethargy and lack of breath. I felt I was dying.

Janet had her heart tested and a brain scan. There were no indications of epilepsy, but they found a blockage in her sinuses which they assumed was caused by an infection and the matter was not pursued.

Researchers investigating other such cases have been exploring the possibility that these blockages are caused by electronic tagging devices inserted by extraterrestrials. Several small metal objects have been discovered, in various parts of the body, but the results of examining them have as yet been inconclusive. A recent case involved objects removed from two unrelated abductees in August

1995 by a surgeon who wishes to remain anonymous.

'Dr X' works in Ventura, California, and the abductees, a man and a woman, were referred to him by a Houston-based ufologist. He removed an object the size of a large seed from the man's hand and a T-shaped object from the woman's big toe. The operations were filmed before witnesses. Each object was encased in a thick, dark membrane.

Dr X told a reporter: 'These weren't cysts. They were so tough my scalpel couldn't cut them. In decades of practice I have never seen anything quite like this.'

When dried out, the objects were cut open to reveal two pieces of highly magnetic, shiny black metal which glowed brilliant green under ultraviolet light.

When Abigail (see Chapter 7) was around seven she was taken to hospital by her mother as a result of inexplicable nosebleeds. A small lozenge-shaped metallic object was retrieved from inside her nose, but unfortunately, it was left with the medical staff and its fate remains unknown.

Years later, in the early hours of 17 April 1996, Abigail got up and went downstairs for a glass of water. Everything seemed quite normal. She went back to bed and slept until 7.55am. When she woke up, the young woman was immediately aware of a pain in her right thigh. Examination of the leg revealed two parallel cuts below the surface of the skin (see plate section). Abigail carefully retraced her steps down to the kitchen, looking for anything that might have caused the strange wound. As it was quite painful, she wondered how it could have happened without her knowledge. Then, after searching her bed as well, she gave up.

Peter Hough examined Abigail's wound two days later. The pain had now subsided but the cuts, apparently beneath the surface of the skin, were still very evident. Two days after that the wound had disappeared altogether.

In another case we investigated, a young man who felt his family were being interfered with by aliens woke up on several occasions with inexplicable marks on his body. One night Stephen Pal woke up screaming, terrified by a dream in which he was being taken somewhere. He found three long scratches and two small ones on his abdomen. Seven months later Stephen showed Peter Hough the scars from these wounds (see plate section). On a later occasion he woke with severe bruising to one of his elbows (see plate section). The type of injury was consistent with being dragged across the floor. There was also a deep scratch on the inside of the same arm.

The morning after Janet and Harry's experience, Harry noticed a curious indentation in his leg. It reminded him of a television aerial socket, except that the mark was square, not round. In an attempt to rationalize it, Harry conjectured that he must have banged his leg on something during the night on his way back to bed after visiting the bathroom. The mark faded within a few days.

At around the same time the couple had an identical dream, on the same night. Harry told us: 'I hardly ever dream of spacecraft. It's not something I would think about. We'd been in a crowd watching the Tall Ships, and we were in a crowd during the dream, being "beamed up" into a circular object.'

Janet added: 'We both experienced movement in the dream, as if we were in something, going somewhere. When we awoke we both rushed to the bathroom and threw up. We felt sick, had headaches and were hot.'

Did their attendance at the Tall Ships Parade stimulate a fantasy? How could both of them have experienced an identical dream on the same night and suffered the same spontaneous physiological effects? The phenomenon of shared delusions, referred to as *folie à deux*, is stretched to breaking-point as a simplistic explanation for these cases. As an added complication, Janet told us that her brother's girlfriend was experiencing almost identical dreams during the same period.

Janet's illness, which started the morning after the Tall Ships Parade, resulted in extreme measures being taken.

The doctor and I agreed on a termination of the pregnancy due to ill health, and afterwards the symptoms gradually abated. I felt they were hormonal in origin. Previously the pill had caused similar effects, but less so. I developed an acute allergy to caffeine, alcohol and other stimulants – for no obvious reason. I am not a hypochondriac. It is strange how it ties in with the experience. Had an adjustment been made somehow to my hormones? Is that why I conceived? (We did make love that night.) Was it no more than a dream from my subconscious, a way of telling me I had just become pregnant? That would be incredible in itself!

At the time she was very ill, Janet experienced what she calls a 'blue dream':

I felt I'd been taken somewhere, into a calm blueness inside something round. The beings were getting me to walk through solid objects. When I tried it felt like a coldness enveloped me, and I thought I was going to get stuck, but I didn't. They comforted me as I did it.

Exactly three months after the initial experience Janet woke at 3 am and sensed presences in the room. Again she was sleeping with her boyfriend.

They arrived with a rustling noise. I was aware of three beings around me. They moved closer to the bed and I felt this incredible sensation of moving at speed, as if they were trying to pull me away from Harry. If I let go I felt I would die. I tried to scream and wake him up, but he wouldn't. Then I heard them say, 'She's awake!' They didn't seem too pleased with me. I felt they were angry because the baby was no longer there. I won the struggle and fell asleep.

Unexplained pregnancies are a feature of many American abduction cases. Usually the foetus 'inexplicably' disappears when it is a few weeks or months old. Some investigators, such as Budd Hopkins and Dr David Jacobs, believe that men and women are abducted for experimental purposes: extraterrestrials are extracting sperm and ova which are then used to revitalize the aliens' exhausted gene pool. They create hybrid beings who are incubated in the host Earth mother. When this initial stage is complete, the pregnant woman is re-abducted and the foetus is removed and brought to its full term using alien technology. Sometimes these abductees describe strange dreams where they are shown their hybrid offspring.

Joyce Bond (see Chapter 8) had three dreams concerning babies during the time we were using hypnosis to explore her case. In the first she was holding on her lap a small child who was burying its head in her bare stomach. The second dream was more bizarre:

I was in a large gathering of people. I took an interest in a puppy which belonged to a woman, picked it up and carried it around. It was really sweet with black shiny curly fur, like a spaniel. As I held it up against my shoulder it began speaking in a very clear voice. Nobody seemed to think this was odd. I can't remember what it said, though it was important.

At some stage the puppy seems to have become a baby, wearing a long white Christening dress. I carried it around. It belonged to a middle-aged man. When I took it back we noticed it had stopped breathing. I thought it had died and it was my fault. But the man was not unduly worried and said this had happened before. He started squeezing the baby and it revived.

In the final dream Joyce was looking after a baby. It had a diagonal cut across each knee. These were surgical cuts, and they were stitched.

The notion that extraterrestrials are breeding hybrid beings seems like a bad plot for a low-budget sci-fi film. It couldn't be true . . . could it? In traditional folklore a changeling is the offspring of a fairy, secretly substituted for a human child, a cuckoo destined to influence human society.

A common folk story featuring the birth of a hybrid child involves a midwife who is called out by an ugly old man. She is taken to a strange cottage where a young girl is in labour. The bed is surrounded by small children. As the baby is born the midwife recognizes the mother as a girl who was abducted from the village some time before. Then she sees her surroundings as they really are: the cottage is a cave, the children are hairy imps and the old man is even uglier than before.

Such folk tales have strong parallels with contemporary abduction experiences. The cave in the story above, for example would now be a dome-shaped UFO and the hairy imps aliens. The girl had been used to breed a hybrid child.

It came as no surprise to learn that Janet and Harry could relate previous encounters from childhood. Janet, like Abigail and a significant number of other abductees, can remember back to babyhood. Research in the USA has confirmed that abductees have better-than-average recall of events which happened very early in their lives. Janet reminds her mother that she used to scream when having her nappy changed because 'I didn't like my legs being lifted up'. She could read at the age of three and a half and today is a member of MENSA. Janet has some vivid memories of things which happened while she was a small child.

She remembers lying in her cot and seeing four small white figures walking around the room. These were her 'friends'. Under hypnosis she described them as small, like eight-year-old children, with pale, hairless skin. Janet told us: 'They are made; they're not what you see.' One friend in particular was special, and used to hold Janet's hand as she lay in the cot. Its hand felt cold.

These beings used to take Janet somewhere in a blaze of light. Then she would be left alone with a tall man wearing a hat and coat. Some sort of procedure would follow where she felt something being put inside her. Janet was to meet that man again, although she would not remember her childhood encounters.

Under hypnosis Janet described how, when she was four years old, her friends would play games in her bedroom. The following is an extract from the transcript of the recording of this session:

KALMAN: *What are your friends doing?*
JANET: *Playing with toys.*
KALMAN: *Do you play together?*
JANET: *I'm on the bed, watching. I should be asleep.*
HOUGH: *What toys are they playing with? Can you describe them?*
JANET: *Black boxes, four. They make me feel happy.*
HOUGH: *Can you touch them?*
JANET: *Mustn't touch them. Hurt.*
KALMAN: *What happens when the friends touch the boxes?*
JANET: *They understand them better.*

She then describes how they sometimes took her away to 'the playroom' which is 'up there'. She says she gets there by flying. The entities sometimes allow her to travel to her favourite place, Abersoch, in Wales. In the playroom she meets other children, but none of them talk to one another. They just sit while the beings show them 'pictures' of the Earth and tell them that it is at risk of destruction. Janet also recollects a figure coming down through the ceiling, which she described at the time as 'a witch or a wizard'. She told us:

I was frantic and told Mum I didn't want to be in the cot any more as I felt trapped. I was not dreaming. I never saw things which weren't there. I had terrible nosebleeds, as did my mother. She doesn't have them any more, but I still do.

The fact that Janet's mother also suffered nosebleeds supports the theory that whole families are targeted and the abductions take place over generations. Janet claims she sometimes wakes up at three in the morning with a bloody nose and a feeling that something has happened which she has forgotten.

Janet and her parents often used to caravan in Wales when she was a child. When she was about 11 she took a friend with her. One day the two girls went out for a long walk. On their way back, dusk seemed to fall unexpectedly early. As they passed a church the girls noticed a man dressed in black, wearing a cape and hat. He vanished as they looked at him. Back at the caravan, they discovered it was after 11 pm. They had set off at six for a walk which should have lasted no more than an hour and a half. Janet told us the walk had been her idea, adding that she often has strong urges to go for walks in isolated areas at the strangest hours.

Janet claims that she, her mother, her brother and her brother's girlfriend are regularly mistaken for someone else, or are told by people they know that they have a double. When they attempt to track down the double something invariably goes wrong and they are prevented from finding them.

She has also been plagued with silent telephone calls. One evening she went out for dinner with her brother and his girlfriend. When they came back to the flat Jane realized that one of her earrings was missing. They made a thorough search of the flat and even went back to the restaurant to see if anyone had handed in the earring, to no avail. At 11 pm the telephone rang. Janet recalls:

I got up to answer it. There was nobody there so I dialled 1471, but no number was stored. As I put the phone down something came over me. I looked at my brother's girlfriend and said, 'The earring's back.' She picked her hand up off the settee, and it was underneath.

The curious 'dream' that eight-year-old Harry once experienced in the dentist's chair 'was probably the most vivid thing that ever happened to me in my whole life', he told us.

That day Harry was due to have a couple of baby teeth taken out, which had been troubling him. As he lay back nervously in the chair, the young dental nurse took hold of his hand to comfort him.

'I knew I had to have the gas,' he explained. 'They put a mask over my face and the smell of rubber was nauseating. Someone told me to count to ten, and before I had finished I was gone.'

In the ensuing dream the little boy was somewhere else and five years old. He re-experienced it for us under hypnosis:

I am on a sort of table and can't move my arms. There is the same bright white light there was in the dentist's. Three 'people' are standing around me. One of them is holding my hand, just like the nurse in the dentist's room. She – I think it is a she – is on my right-hand side. This being seems to be a guide or caretaker.

There is a sense of intent. They've got a job to do and they'll just get on with it. I feel calm, with just a mild interest. I can't actually see what is being done. I think they are working on my head. There is a slight feeling of a scalpel at work.

Then Harry remembers standing at a window – one of many punched into the wall of the circular room – and looking down at the ground. Something causes him to turn around:

My attention is drawn towards a long, slim glass tube with sparks arcing across in it. It's a cutting thing. There's a girl. I know her face. She's very nice, brunette. Beings in white gowns are helping her off the table. They're holding her hands. I think she recognizes me. She looks like a girl from my class at school, Barbara Kerr. Barbara's a subject for what they can do. It's some sort of experiment to make her special, wiser.

Harry also recalls seeing a UFO:

[The UFO] was very stereotyped, with lots of portholes and a turret, but elegantly constructed. The portholes were spinning as it took off. As I came out of the gas the object was spinning and so was the being who was holding my hand in the dream.

Harry went on to describe an incident that took place two years later, during a lesson at school. Barbara is only seven, but she starts to have a period in class, and the teacher takes her away. Harry understands what is happening. As she passes him he wants to put his arms around Barbara and comfort her.

The sceptic in us wants to explain Harry's 'dream' as a simple reflection of Harry's real-life predicament in the dentist's surgery, but it seems very detailed for a reflection, and the explanation can just as easily be turned on its head. Believers will say that the circumstances in the dentist's surgery so closely mirrored a suppressed memory that it resurfaced. Harry voiced similar feelings:

I'm not entirely convinced that the dream was just a dream. There was a sense that it was near to something which had actually happened. I could never explain to myself why it was so vivid, why it felt so real.

What does Janet believe lies behind her abduction experiences? 'They seem to want to make changes in us, to put things right,' she says. 'And what they do seems very natural.'

Moyshe Kalman observed that both Janet and Harry presented themselves for exploration with a certain eagerness. He noted they were 'look-alikes' and could pass for siblings, both being fair and overweight, and came from similar social backgrounds. Harry seemed more confident than Janet, who showed some embarrassment in speaking seriously about encounter experiences.

Janet had a good job and a high IQ and seemed a very competent woman. The 'aliens' had been her only friends from earliest childhood and had given her life meaning. She revealed that they had presented her with a philosophy which laid bare the substance of the world, although, as is usual in these cases, their 'wisdom' appeared rather banal, like New Age idealism. This was perhaps an attempt to mask the serious and sinister aspects of Janet and Harry's experiences.

Chapter 4

The Green Man

This thing happened to me on 1 December 1987. It was dark and overcast when I set off from home around quarter past seven in the morning to cross the moors for East Morton, the village where my father-in-law lived. I brought a camera, hoping to take some shots of Ilkley from the moor tops. Up there it's surprisingly easy to get disorientated if the weather turns bad. I had completed the 5-mile walk once or twice before, but this time I carried a compass with me. As an experienced walker you take no chances in winter.

Rather than follow the established path, I took the shorter, though more arduous route, up the face of the steep hillside. As the ground started to level out I picked up a path which ran alongside a stand of trees. There was a humming which I assumed was from an aircraft hidden in the overcast sky.

Then something caught my eye. I stopped and turned, looking into a huge hollow scooped out of the top of the hill. About 20 feet away I saw, what I can only describe as a small green creature, moving quickly deeper into the hollow. I thought, What's that? and shouted, 'Hey!'. When it was about 40 to 50 feet away it turned and seemed to be waving me off. I quickly brought up the camera and took a photograph. Then, I don't know why exactly, I jumped down the embankment and chased after it.

It didn't walk so much as shamble, but nevertheless moved much more quickly than was normal. I followed it around an out-cropping. There was a deeper excavation and an even bigger surprise.

I saw a large object like two silver saucers stuck together edge *to edge. A box sticking out of the top was descending into the object, and the humming I had previously heard became quite loud, then the 'saucer' shot straight up into the clouds.*

Confused, I came back down off the moors into Ilkley. The shops were open and the church clock said it was ten. I realized it should only have been about eight fifteen! I could not account for one and three-quarter hours.

Was I going mad? Had I suffered a breakdown up on the moors? Then I remembered the photograph. There was a place in nearby Keighley which operated a one-hour processing service. I caught the next bus and walked the short distance to the shop, taking a couple of shots as I went. I felt guilty at wasting so much film, then realized the futility of it.

Returning to the shop I nervously took out the handful of prints, and there it was. The quality was poor, but there was no doubt I had captured on film what I had seen with my own eyes: a small green creature, arm bent, waving me away.

The above account, compiled from letters and recorded interviews, was made by a former police officer using the pseudonym 'Philip Spencer'. Spencer offered investigators more than a story of a UFO encounter. He showed us the photograph and his compass. The young man discovered after the incident that the compass was now 'totally inaccurate'. The polarity of the compass had been reversed, so that it pointed south instead of north. It was a sealed unit, so tampering was highly unlikely. Spencer had been using Kodacolor VR 400 ASA film that day up on the Yorkshire moors. The picture (see plate section) was both intriguing and disappointing. It did indeed show a small green figure standing in a large hollow, but the photograph was grainy and lacking in fine detail. However, it was possible to see the figure had a long body, short thin legs and very long arms. Was this case an elaborate hoax, or one that proved the objective reality of alien encounters? Spencer's answer to the suggestion was forthright and without malice:

I'm not particularly interested in what other people think. I know what I saw, and if people don't believe me that's up to them. I've got nothing to gain by doing that. I don't see the sense; I've got better things to do with my time.

Indeed, Spencer does seem to have nothing to gain from faking an encounter. From the start he insisted that his true identity never be revealed because 'It would ruin me socially and professionally'. Neither has he sought to profit financially from the story, although money was offered by several media sources. When Nippon Television filmed the story, Spencer refused a fee, reluctantly accepting a small gift instead.

Spencer's camera was an old 35 mm Dixons' own brand called a PRINZ Mastermatic, a very basic lightweight instrument without a focusing screen or SLR (single lens reflex) facilities. It had a 45 mm lens and an integral light meter, which had not worked for a number of years. The camera was composed largely of plastic and neither it nor the film had been affected in any way by their proximity to the alleged 'saucer'.

The photograph featuring the small green figure was the tenth on a 24-exposure roll of film. Only two shots were taken after it, one of some cars on a road and the other of Keighley bus station, which Philip took only because he didn't want to waste the rest of the film. The remaining 12 frames were unused.

Considering the very basic camera design and non-functioning light meter, Peter Hough was surprised when Spencer showed him the other prints from the film. Most of them were clear, well-composed scenic shots taken on previous occasions. By far the worst picture was the one of the 'creature'– the most important one of all. This was dark and grainy. Why?

According to Spencer, he had pre-set the camera for the sort of low-light conditions he expected on the moor before he left home. Thinking back later on, he could not be certain about the exact settings, but he knew he had set the film at a low speed, and the aperture at 2.8 (the camera's widest aperture) or 4. Given these settings and the 400 ASA film, Spencer should been able to take a fairly clear photograph, if the time was as reported: around 7.45 am.

Was the time correct? In the photograph, the sky above the horizon is light, not dark and overcast as Spencer had described. On 1 December, sunrise was at 7.57 am. Yet it is just half an hour's walk from Spencer's house to that spot on the moor.

There is even more in the photograph than is at first apparent. Although Spencer apparently had not noticed it, to the right of the 'creature', above and behind the outcrop is the faint image of a squarish object. At first glance it would seem to be in the right place to confirm Spencer's story of observing a box disappearing into the 'saucer'. Had he also captured part of the UFO on film? An examination of the site revealed no natural rock formation to account for the object in the photograph.

Twelve months after the incident came a breakthrough. Investigators Philip Mantle and Andy Roberts went up to the location around the anniversary of the encounter. They took lots of photographs and on two of them appeared a box-like shape. It was not as prominent as on the original, but nevertheless it was in exactly the same place. It seemed to be some sort of reflection from the far bank of the outcrop. Roberts speculated that the effect was brought about at that time of the year when the moisture content of the ground and the lighting conditions were exactly right. Further, the effect was visible only from the exact spot where the original picture had been taken. What bearing did this have on the case?

While it is true that Spencer never put forward the image as further proof of his encounter – in fact, the image is too far off-centre to correspond with his 'saucer' – Andy Roberts believed here was proof that the former police officer had hoaxed the picture. He suggested that, after photographing a dummy, Spencer had noticed the faint image in the background, and woven it into his story, then he had sat back and waited for investigators to notice it. This is a plausible idea, except that the image does not quite fit Spencer's description of the box. In a letter to ufologist Jenny Randles dated 3 December 1987, he described it as 'a square box with holes'.

Jenny Randles and Peter Hough took the print and negative to the professional wildlife photographer Tony Marshall for evaluation. Tony was not impressed by the poor quality of the picture and wondered, somewhat critically, why pictures of the 'unknown' are often blurred and indistinct. He thought that the faint white image might have been caused by a tiny scratch on the negative which diffused the light when it was exposed.

The director of a small photographic laboratory in Manchester studied the negative and print with some scepticism. He thought the print was too grainy even for 400 ASA film and wondered whether it might not be an original, but a photograph of a photograph. There was some slight 'flaring' along the bottom of the print and up either side which, he speculated, could be indicative of a badly placed lighting source. He also noted that the print was slightly out of focus. Some hoaxers have deliberately employed these techniques to hide details which might 'give the game away'.

Peter Sutherst at Kodak gave us his expert advice after examining the negative:

It [the exposure] *is underexposed by at least two stops. It is usual for these films to produce grainy pictures when underexposed. The negative shows a degree of camera shake, making it difficult to decide what the small figure might be. Identification is made even more of a problem because of underexposure.*

I would not care to commit myself to any observation beyond saying that the film had not been interfered with after processing.

He added that this was not a photograph of a photograph and the slight flaring was due to poor-quality film processing. The figure – whatever it was – was actually there at the site where it was photographed.

Over the years there has been a lot of talk about computer image enhancement of the photograph. This involves sharpening up photographic images by using a computer to detect patterns and fill in the missing pixels. In 1988 Peter Sutherst made these comments on the subject:

Image enhancement is a costly exercise and I have some doubt about the benefits in this case. The size, distance of the subject, camera movement and underexposure mean that there is insufficient detail available to enhance.

Geoffrey Crawley of the *British Journal of Photography* attempted computer enhancement of the photograph in 1990 (see plate section). Some years earlier Crawley had helped prove that the famous 'Cottingley fairies' photographed by Elsie Wright and Frances Griffiths were cardboard cut-outs. Unfortunately his work on Spencer's picture met with failure. Attempts in Japan also failed to clarify the image.

When Nippon Television visited England in May 1989, Peter Hough was witness to a remarkable demonstration of Japanese improvisation. The photograph was stuck to a wall and a very bright studio lamp positioned to illuminate it. Then a television camera was focused on the picture and the image fed directly to a 15-cm (6-inch) monitor, which had the effect of highlighting the contrast between the figure and the background. This cleared up another of the mysteries surrounding the photograph.

The left arm of the 'creature' ends in an amorphous mass. Some commentators have speculated that the figure is carrying something. Even Geoffrey Crawley thought he could make out the outline of something resembling a briefcase in his computer enhancements. The Japanese film crew demonstrated that this was caused by the entity's hand and the ground directly behind it merging together. On the small monitor the outline of a hand, with three fingers, could clearly be seen.

Apart from the camera shake and underexposure, there is another reason why the figure is so hard to define. It is almost camouflaged into the environment. Is this subtlety something a hoaxer would incorporate, or does it tell us more about the phenomenon?

Peter Hough arranged with Professor Raymond Leonard, head of the Total Technology Department at the University of Manchester Institute of Science and Technology (UMIST), to carry out some work on Spencer's compass. On 19 January 1988 Hough and investigator Arthur Tomlinson had a meeting with Dr Spooner, head of the Department of Electrical Engineering and Electronics at UMIST. It was to prove a very interesting morning.

Just how could the polarity of a compass be reversed? Dr Spooner began by simply exposing the compass to some very strong magnets. Although they deflected the needle, the effect ceased as soon as the magnets were removed. A steady magnetic field, it seemed, had no permanent effect. Dr Spooner and his assistant then experimented with a 'pulsed', or rapidly applied magnetic field. Eventually it was found that this would reverse the needle, and reverse it back again, under laboratory controlled conditions.

This was interesting, but could the reversal be brought about without recourse to such expensive and complex equipment? Dr Spooner showed that it could, albeit with a certain risk to life and property. It was decided to create an electromagnetic field inside a coil of wire. The ends of the wire were connected to the mains electricity supply and a switch on the wall was thrown. There was a bang and a fuse blew, but yes, the polarity of the compass changed from north to south. Spooner concluded that the same effect could be brought about using a car battery.

Dr Spooner had demonstrated that a compass could be reversed by trickery. However, this would entail the risk of injury or fire and would be impossible without the necessary scientific knowledge. In his report, Dr Spooner wrote:

It appears to be a relatively simple matter to bring about the reversal without the need for any special equipment and it may be accomplished in the average home or garage. The intensity required is not great by some standards; in fact we could not produce a field sufficiently low as not to reverse the polarity of the needle. The minimum field we applied had a flux density of about 0.1 Tesla; this is still about 2000 times greater than the Earth's field. . . . [Therefore] the required intensity is very large by other standards to leave detectable magnetization in samples of rock.

Dr Spooner went on to say that perhaps one way of determining evidence 'for or against the claim' would be to carry out a magnetic survey of the surrounding rocks. If a powerful magnetic field associated with the 'saucer' had affected the compass, it would also have affected the immediate environment, assuming that the compass had been affected near the ground. However, the magnetic survey suggested by Spooner was felt to be unnecessary after subsequent events.

Peter Hough took Liz Kelly of the Radiological Protection Service, based at the University of Manchester, up to Ilkley Moor. Liz carried out a radiation survey of the location and took away grass and soil samples for further analysis. Some witnesses of close-encounter experiences have exhibited symptoms of radiation exposure and Philip Spencer had complained of headaches for a week after his experience. In this case, however, only normal background radiation was detected.

In March 1988 Spencer asked Peter Hough whether he could be hypnotized, as he had began to feel that this would enhance his memory of the missing one hour and three-quarters. He had recently experienced a vivid dream where he was staring at a pattern of stars in the sky and thought this might be significant.

The investigators were put in touch with Jim Singleton, a clinical psychologist with a practice at a major hospital in the North of England. Jim was open-minded enough to take part in the investigation and agreed to interview Spencer under hypnosis. Here is a full transcript of the session:

SINGLETON: *I want you now to cast your mind back to the first of December last year when you set off across the moor. I want you to cast your mind back to that and I want you to re-experience that. I want you to tell me what you experienced.*

SPENCER: *I'm walking along the moor. Oh! It's quite windy. There's a lot of cloud. Walking up towards the trees, I see this little something, can't tell, but he's green. It's moving towards me. Oh! I can't move, I'm stuck! He's still coming towards me. And I still can't move. . . . I'm stuck, and everything's gone fuzzy. I'm . . . I'm floating along in the air . . . I want to get down! And this green thing's walking ahead of me, and I don't like it. I still can't move, I'm going round the corner and this green thing's in front of me. Oh God. . . . I want to get down!*

[Long pause.] *There's a . . .* [Breathing faster] *there's a big silver, like, saucer thing, and there's a door in it, and I don't want to go in there!* [Sounds worried. Sighs.] *Everything's gone black now.* [Pause.]

SINGLETON: *You say everything's gone black?*

SPENCER: *Mmm. I can't see anything, like I'm asleep, can't hear anything.* [Short pause.] *There's a bright light now, can't see where it's coming from. I'm in a funny sort of room. I can hear this voice saying, 'Don't be afraid.' I don't feel afraid any more. I can still see this green thing, but I'm not frightened of it now.* [Murmurs something.]

I'm being put onto a table. I can move now if I want to, but I don't feel frightened. And there's a beam like a pole, it's above me, it's moving up towards me, it's got a light in it. Like a fluorescent tube. It's coming up from my feet. I can hear that voice again saying, 'We don't mean to harm you and don't be afraid.'

Makes me feel warm as it's moving up me. It's coming up over my stomach, towards my head. Close my eyes. I don't want to look at it in case it hurts my eyes. It's gone. [Pause.]

There's something. My nose feels uncomfortable. *That's gone as well. I'm standing up now. I don't know how I got stood up. I can see a door. There's one of these green creatures motioning for me to come with him. Don't really want to go with him. I'd rather stay here. I don't feel afraid in here....*

SINGLETON: *Can you tell me what's happening now?*

SPENCER: *I'm walking towards a door. There's still a bright light. I can't see where it's coming from. There's light all around. Want to know where the light is. It's just bright, it's just light. Walking down a corridor, there's a window. Oh! God!* [Sounds shocked.] *Is that real?* [Deep sigh, then a pause. He explained afterwards that he could see the Earth as if from space at this point.] *Don't want to be up here – I want to be down there.* [Sounds afraid.] *I can hear that voice again, saying, 'You've got nothing to fear.' It's pretty, though. Didn't realize it looks so pretty. I've gone past the window now; I'm walking down a corridor.* [Long pause.]

SINGLETON: *What's happening now?*

SPENCER: *Come to the end of the corridor. There's a hole opened in it so I can walk through. I'm in a big room, a big round room. I'm on a raised platform against the wall. My camera and compass are trying to get away from me,* [These were hanging from cords around his neck.] *going towards the ball. It's difficult to pull them back down again. And this ball's moving round, with things around it. Looks strange; it's got some blocks on it. He says we can't stay in here long. He wants us to go out again. The hole's closed in the wall.* [Pause.] *It's gone strange. He says I've got nothing to fear, but I'd like to go home.* [Pause.] *It's got such big hands.* [Long pause.]

SINGLETON: *What's happening now?*

SPENCER: *Going down a corridor again. It's very bright still. I wish I knew where the light was coming from. And there's another door. Going through a door; it's an empty room. Two of those green creatures have come with me. There's a picture, it's starting to move on the wall.* [Pause.] *Wonder how they get the pictures?*

SINGLETON: *Can you tell me what's happening at this point?*

SPENCER: *I'm looking at the pictures on the wall.* [Long pause.]

SINGLETON: *Pictures on the wall?*

SPENCER: *Mmm!* [Pause.] *Creatures seem concerned at the damage that it's doing. Pictures changing now, there's another picture, another film.* [Pause.] *He's asking me a question. He says, 'Do you understand?' I said 'Yes'.* [Long pause.] *It's time to go. Everything's gone black. I'm walking up the moor again now. I'm walking up near some trees. Some movement – I can see something. A green creature. I've shouted to it. It's turned round. I don't know what it is. I'll photograph it. It's turned around now. It's moving quick. Want to know what it is. I'm running after it! It's gone round a corner, I can't see it now. There's . . . there's a saucer!* [Laughing.] *Big silver saucer! It's disappeared.* [Pause.] *I'm walking on down, gone past the trees.* [Long pause.]

SINGLETON: *What's happening now?*

SPENCER: *I'm going home. It's ten o'clock on the town hall. Can't really understand. It was only eight o'clock.* [Pause.]

SINGLETON: *Now, is there anything else you want to say about this last event?*

SPENCER: *No.*

SINGLETON: *Would you mind if I asked you one or two questions?*

SPENCER: *No.*

SINGLETON: *You mentioned some green creatures. Would you try to describe one of them to me?*

SPENCER: *It's quite small. He's got big pointed ears; it's got big eyes. They're quite dark. He hasn't got a nose. He's only got a little mouth. And his hands are enormous. And his arms are long. He's got funny feet.*

SINGLETON: *Funny feet?*

SPENCER: *They're like a V-shape, like two big toes.* [Short pause.] *Must be difficult to walk like that. He shuffles rather than walks. I don't feel afraid of him, although he looks odd.*

SINGLETON: *You mentioned big hands. Can you say anything more about the hands?*

SPENCER: *It's got three big fingers, like sausages. Big sausages. They're just very big. Bigger than my hands.*

SINGLETON: *About how tall would you say these creatures are, roughly?*

SPENCER: *It's about four foot. Comes to the lump on my stomach, he's about as high as my – just a bit bigger than my stomach is.*

SINGLETON: *Is there anything else you'd like to say about this creature?*

SPENCER: *I don't think so.*

SINGLETON: *No? OK. Now, I wonder if I can ask you another question. You mention watching a film?*

SPENCER: *Mmm.*

SINGLETON: *Could you say anything more about the film you didn't say to me at the time? What the content of the film was – can you say anything more about that?*

SPENCER: *There were two films.*

SINGLETON: *Two films?*

SPENCER: *One was lots of scenes of destruction, like on the news. Can see lots of waste going into the river. And people like Ethiopians who are starving. It's not very good, it's not very nice.*

SINGLETON: *Want to say anything more about that film?*

SPENCER: *It's much of the same thing, only different.*

SINGLETON: *What about the other film, then? Do you want to tell me about that?*

SPENCER: *I'm not supposed to.*

SINGLETON: *I'll leave that up to you entirely. Do you want to say anything about it?*

SPENCER: *I'm not supposed to tell anybody about the other film.*

SINGLETON: *You're not supposed to tell anyone about the other film?*

SPENCER: *[Whispers.] No.*

SINGLETON: *Do you want to tell anyone about the other film or not?*

SPENCER: *No, it's not for them to know.*

SINGLETON: *OK. Now, is there anything else that you would like to add to what you've already told me?*

SPENCER: *I don't think so.*

SINGLETON: *OK.*

Spencer's hypnosis testimony contained many of the elements of other abduction reports: small alien beings; a bench in the middle of the examination room; physical examination; white light from no obvious source; a tour around the ship; ecological warnings. There was also an indication that the beings were doing something to his nose.

How did Jim Singleton feel about Philip's story? Jim said he found him to be a good hypnotic subject, perhaps slightly better than most. Was Spencer really hypnotized?

I think he was definitely under hypnosis. That's my opinion. To have faked it convincingly, Philip would have had to have studied hours of videotaped sessions. Then he would have to be a very good actor to have carried it off. I think the hypnosis was genuine.

He was certainly recounting the incident as something which had actually happened. He described things typically as someone would recall a past event. He compares very well with other non-UFO subjects.

When asked about hypnosis as a tool to uncovering the truth, Singleton replied:

Experimental studies suggest that people can modify or vary their recall, so obviously there is no certainty that what is recalled under hypnosis is 100 per cent. However, here I think I've helped Philip to recover memories that were hidden more deeply in the mind.

Why did Singleton think they were hidden in the first place?

In terms of my clinical work, if people experience things which are unusual, traumatic or frightening, the mind protects itself by pushing them deep into the subconscious. People that way don't recall them immediately. Hypnosis seems to lower the threshold of this barrier.

How then did Singleton view Spencer's photograph? This was the pivotal point of the entire case. If the picture was genuine, the speculation that UFO abductions were a purely psychological phenomenon would be refuted. Either the picture was genuine, in which case we were dealing with a real abduction, or it was a fake, which would mean we had all been wasting our time. Jim Singleton had no doubts:

It seems – there again – very consistent. I suppose the good thing about the photograph is it helps Philip face up to a very unusual experience. With the photograph he has some material evidence to back up what he knows as a memory.

While Hough interviewed Singleton, Spencer sat at the back of the room, very quiet and introspective. The psychologist had enabled Spencer to retain a full conscious memory of his hypnosis narrative if he wished. How vivid was his recollection?

'It was very clear' he said. 'I've no trouble remembering what I saw.'

Judging by Spencer's hypnosis testimony, it would seem that the photograph was taken at the end of the experience. This would explain the missing period of time and the lightness of the sky. (However, if the camera settings were correct, the picture should have been overexposed, not underexposed.) It would seem – if we take his story at face value – that the polarity of Spencer's compass was reversed while he was inside a spacecraft orbiting the Earth.

The questions now centred on the paralysis which had stopped him fleeing back down the hill. He replied:

I was quite conscious of the fact I couldn't move, conscious of where I was going and the creature in front of me. I was 'floating', still standing upright, and felt much like a bear on the end of a piece of invisible rope.

After the hypnosis session Spencer supplied Hough with further material regarding the creatures and his 'abduction'. (It is not uncommon for further 'memories' to surface after hypnosis.) He said their skin was green and pitted, almost reptilian, and there was no evidence of genitals, or gender. Their eyes were large, round and dark; he said they were 'kind', and gave the impression they could see into his mind.

'The creatures seemed part of a team,' he said. 'They weren't acting as individuals but more like bees, as if they were doing what they were programmed to do.'

Many other 'abductees', including American abductee Whitley Strieber, have likened their abductors' behaviour to that of robots, ants or bees. But Spencer also received this impression:

I had a feeling of goodness about these creatures. I don't think they would harm anybody. I would go so far, in retrospect, to say I actually liked them. I certainly felt no threat from them after the onset of the meeting.

He could not recollect any sounds in the object he entered, even his own footsteps, except a humming in the background. The beings communicated with him by means of telepathy. Although many aspects of his experience were common to other cases, and had been reported in the media, there were some, which in 1988, had not received much publicity.

For example, during the abduction, Spencer remarked that his nose 'felt funny'. In January 1994, he told Peter Hough: 'Over the last few years I've had quite a few spontaneous nosebleeds. I've had my nose cauterized twice, with various degrees of success.'

Also, it is only in the last few years that investigators have talked about 'doorway amnesia'. Spencer described seeing a door open in the object, but he could not actually recollect going through it – just the onset of blackness followed by an awareness of being in the white room. He could not have taken that idea from a book. Whenever people are asked to imagine an abduction by aliens, they inevitably describe being taken up some sort of ramp into the spaceship. Abductees almost never say how they actually went into the craft to which they were taken.

We knew that the first film shown to Spencer depicted a warning of ecological disaster, but what about the second film, which Jim Singleton had failed to get him to elaborate on? Spencer still will not discuss it, except to say it was of a very personal nature.

'If you're married you will understand,' he explained. 'There are certain things about your wife you would never tell anyone. And that's how I feel about the second film.'

On another occasion Spencer did tell Peter Hough that he did not expect to live to see his fortieth birthday. Similarly, in 1995 postman Henry Tate, another abductee, said: 'I feel like I haven't got long to live'; Abigail (see Chapter 7) spoke of her conviction that she would die before she was 40, and Reza did not long survive his experience.

The credibility of abduction cases is often determined by the character of the person concerned. What are we to make of Philip Spencer? Is the photograph a hoax and his story a fabrication? Hough's first impression was that he seemed 'too laid back' about the affair and more interested in the reactions of the investigators than in what he alleged had happened to him. Yet he wanted neither publicity nor money. The hoax hypothesis made sense only if Spencer were a debunker or a front man for a group of debunkers planning to discredit ufology by exposing the fraud after the case had become part of the UFO literature. After almost a decade, no evidence to support this theory has emerged.

Spencer does not seem to attach any value to the photograph, except as a record of his experience. When I told him that, fake or genuine, the picture and story could be sold for thousands of pounds to certain national newspapers, he just shrugged his shoulders as if he did not care, even though he is not financially well off. We have seen that reaction many times before in witnesses. The experience seems to affect them in a very personal manner and it never occurs to them to 'cash in' on it.

Jim Singleton found Spencer to be psychologically sound and commented: 'The only thing I do find odd is how he could ever have become a policeman. Philip seems too sensitive for that role.' He also said:

I think that if people make unusual claims we should at least listen to them, and listen very carefully. We don't know all the answers to everything. If we are going to be even remotely scientific we've got to entertain these different ideas, thoughts and impressions.

In January 1988 Peter Hough asked Spencer's wife what she thought of the photograph. This put her in something of a dilemma. She said she found it unbelievable, yet had always known her husband to be honest. Although we were unaware of it at the time, she made this statement at a point when the couple's marriage was about to end and she therefore had no reason to be loyal to him. They remained good friends after the divorce.

Philip Spencer applied to rejoin the police force, and by way of an independent character assessment, showed Hough a private letter from a serving police officer who had known him for eight years. This letter spoke of Philip's 'good character' and 'honesty'.

In May 1996 Philip informed Hough he was about to emigrate to New Zealand to start a new life. Neither his career nor his private life had revived after the encounter. Before he left we asked him for his latest thoughts on the event, now almost nine years in the past. He wrote:

When I think back to the incident, in some ways it seems like any other episode in my life, just a simple memory. Yet I still find it hard to accept that it actually happened as it was so far removed from normal everyday experience. Although, of course, I know that it did happen.

I live my life in much the same way as before. I get on with life the same as anybody else, struggle with the same things, and have the same problems. Although I have changed over the years, hopefully for the better, I think this is due to the natural passage of time and learning rather than due to any aspect of the incident.

One thing has changed which I feel might be due to the experience. I now question everything, and every aspect of everything. It has made me a much more sceptical person. I feel I have been dropped into a sea of uncertainty, unable now to have a belief in anything. What happened to me on the moors was 'impossible'. It throws everything which you think is normal, certain and secure into question. I now exist in a vacuum of disbelief, occasionally reaching out to hold onto something solid, only to discover it is a hologram.

I don't live in fear that 'they' will return, although I do find myself looking up at the sky some nights, thinking deeply. I have no set ideas on where 'they' came from. I prefer to remain objective than to allow myself to become a 'believer'. I am certain however that it was a real objective experience, and I'm glad I have the photograph to remind me that it wasn't simply something like a dream.

Why did it happen to me? I remember a scene from the Disney film Flight of the Navigator *where a young boy is taken away by a small spacecraft. He asks it why it chose him. The robot replies*

'Why not?', *which is perhaps fair comment. Many of us have the habit of saying* 'Why me?' *when something unusual happens, but as Forrest Gump said:* 'Life is like a box of chocolates; you never know what you're gonna get.'

I cannot say that I have gained any unique insight into anything because of the experience, nor that I now have answers to things which evaded me before. I think it was just a random event. Maybe I was just in the wrong place at the wrong time, and that's what came up when I dipped my hand in the 'box of chocolates'.

Chapter 5

It Looks like a Demon

W hen Peter Hough asked Mrs Spencer what she thought of the small green figure in her husband's photograph, she replied: 'It looks like a demon, doesn't it?' When Spencer was asked under hypnosis to describe the entities who abducted him, he said of their feet, 'They're like a V-shape, like two big toes.' What, one may wonder, is an extraterrestrial doing with cloven hooves?

Remove the UFO trappings and in a former age the experience would have been perceived as a close encounter with a demon. Indeed, it is not the first time that alien creatures have been encountered on Ilkley Moor.

The White Wells building stands on the moor less than 500 m (450 yd) from where Philip Spencer had his experiences. It is con-structed around a natural spring and was bequeathed to the people of Ilkley at the beginning of the nineteenth century. A bathman called William Butterfield used to be employed to open the premises. One morning in 1815 he put his key in the lock and it spun around of its own accord. Butterfield later described to a local man what he saw when he looked inside:

All over the water and dipping into it was a lot of little creatures dressed in green, none more than eighteen inches high, making a chatter and a jabber. They seemed to be taking a bath, only they bathed with all their clothes on. Soon, however, one or two of them began to make off, bounding over the walls like squirrels. Then the whole tribe went, helter skelter, toppling and tumbling, heads over heels. The sight was so unusual, that he declared he couldn't, or daren't attempt to rush after them.

One wonders if Mr Butterfield 'couldn't' chase them because he was paralysed?

A recently reported encounter with a goblin-like creature took place on 27 September 1995 at Grimsby, South Humberside. After 35-year-old Paul Gilman had fallen out with his mother he temporarily moved into the ground-floor flat of a distant relative called Mike.

Paul was at pains to point out that he, unlike Mike, did not drink. Paul told us: 'I didn't particularly like being there because Mike tends to be awkward, particularly when he's been drinking. He likes cider. On the Wednesday he had drunk two or three large bottles.'

That evening, Mike irritated Paul by talking through a documentary he was watching on television.

'Around 11 pm I decided I'd had enough and in an effort for some peace said I was going to bed,' he said.

In fact, Paul was sleeping on the couch as Mike was staying in the flat's only bedroom. He awoke briefly at about 1 am and noticed that Mike had apparently passed out on the floor. Having drifted off to sleep again, he was woken two hours later by something in the room:

There, bounding towards me from behind an armchair, was a small, ugly being, between three and three and a half feet tall. It ran with a scamper, like the cartoon character Billy Whizz. I tried to move but was paralysed. When I tried to call Mike all I could manage was an incoherent mumble.

The 'being' reached Mike and bent down over him. Then it seemed to realize that Paul was watching. It looked up with an expression of surprise. Then it backed away a few paces, looked once more at Paul and disappeared behind the same chair. Paul immediately regained movement and speech. He woke Mike and asked if he was all right, without explaining his concern. At first Paul had assumed the being was coming for him, but it was quite obvious that Mike was the object of its attention.

Like Spencer's 'creatures', this one had long, thin arms, large pointed ears and huge round eyes set in a triangular head. The whites of its eyes were yellow, however. Paul added:

I don't recall much of its nose or mouth, but it reminded me of a lemur, troll or gnome. It looked like something from folklore, but this was real. The texture of the skin was comparable to skinned, raw chicken, though not as transparent. It was solid enough but a little insubstantial, as if a prod would leave a dimple in it for a while. The colour was puma grey, the grey of old plaster.

When it ran away, its head was turned unnaturally towards me, its chin over its right shoulder. Although the being was agile and fleet, there did appear an almost imperceptible 'animated' motion to its gait, like the stop motion special effects used in old dinosaur and King Kong movies.

Paul never considered that the experience had anything to do with UFOs. No unidentified lights were seen in connection with the being and the encounter did not develop into an abduction. Yet the description and the paralysis are common components in UFO close-encounter experiences. However, it did set Paul speculating along other lines:

I considered that perhaps drinkers like Mike, who claim to sometimes 'see' things coming through walls and so on, attract or manifest beings. Are these heebie-jeebies real somewhere, and attracted to certain states of mind, like those of drunks, drug addicts and the mentally unstable?

Although it had been a frightening and disturbing experience, Paul thought the being was more mischievous than malevolent. Now living back at home again, he still finds it difficult to sleep. To help him feel secure he leaves the television on all night in his room.

Are 'demons' and 'space aliens' one and the same? Comparisons with folklore indicate that they are. Further, the literature clearly illustrates how the root phenomenon adapts to social and individual expectations. This is often referred to as 'cultural tracking'.

A prime example dates from the period between 1880 and 1913, when there were numerous sightings of phantom airships in the USA, Britain and New Zealand. Witnesses described seeing huge propeller-driven objects which were completely silent and had amazing manoeuvrability. At this time, airships were being designed, but none had successfully flown. Close encounters sometimes took place between witnesses and the crews of these craft, who were ordinary-looking men and women wearing clothes compatible with the times. Often they claimed to be secret inventors or military adventurers.

In 1911 an American anthropologist called W. Y. Evans Wentz published his study of fairy traditions and encounters. Much of the material in *The Fairy Faith in Celtic Countries* was derived from firsthand accounts of people who claimed to have met supernatural entities. T. C. Kermode, a member of the Manx Parliament on the Isle of Man, related to Wentz a personal experience:

One October night, I and another young man were going to a kind of harvest-home. My friend happened to look across the river and said:'Oh look, there are the fairies.' I looked across and saw a circle of supernatural light in which spirits became visible. Around the circle I saw come in twos and threes a great crowd of little beings. All of them, who appeared like soldiers, were dressed in red. They moved back and forth amid the circle of light, as they formed into order like troops drilling.

Another witness told Wentz: 'There are as many kinds of fairies as populations in our world. I have seen some who were about two and a half feet high, and some who were as big as we are.'

Another added:

They are able to appear in different forms. One once appeared to me and seemed only four feet high and stoutly built. He said, 'I am bigger than I appear now. We can make the old young, the big small, the small big.'

In short, 'the Gentry', as they were sometimes called, could manifest in a variety of forms, just like today's 'extraterrestrials'. The French physicist Jacques Vallée first developed the theme in his classic work *Passport to Magonia*, published in 1967.

During his abduction in Iran, Simon Taylor was told by the three beings during their journey around the world that 'they, the entities, live here on Earth,' although most humans never encounter them:

'We are not as you see us,' I remember one of them saying. I was unsure how to interpret this, not knowing whether he meant that they were figments of our imagination, or that they existed in a different form, but occasionally materialized in human, or near-human form.

In Chapter 3, Janet said of her 'friends', 'They are made; they're not what you see. Elves were said to live in giant mushrooms, which look remarkably similar to 'flying saucers'. The floor of Simon Taylor's flying craft was covered in a Persian carpet, echoing the tradition of magic carpets in Middle-Eastern mythology. In effect, he and Reza took the modern equivalent of a magic-carpet ride. The lamp which features in Simon's story is an ironic coincidence, too. Or is it all part of an unfathomable game? These are further instances of 'cultural tracking'.

Over the last 30 years the reported descriptions of alleged aliens and UFO occupants have undergone dramatic changes. For example, during the 1960s many troll-like creatures were spotted in South America. In one such case, a saucer-shaped object was seen flying over Pernambuco, Brazil on 26 October 1965. At about noon, Jose Camilho, a mechanic of good repute, was passing along a road through a belt of scrubland when he saw two 'small people' sitting like children on the stump of a fallen banana tree.

As he approached they jumped to their feet and he saw they were less than a metre (3 ft) tall, with shrivelled brown faces, white hair, round, disproportionately large heads and narrow, slanting eyes. One had a sparse beard and wore a dark peaked cap. Camilho noticed that one of the men, who 'looked so astonished it seemed his eyes would leap from their sockets', was carrying a sort of rod, which he indicated to the Brazilian by means of gestures, was a weapon.

The second seemed much calmer. He was wearing a shirt, trousers, footwear similar to tennis shoes and an astonishing luminous belt with an array of bright flashing lights. Between the little men stood a cylinder the same height as them. The one with the luminous belt staggered off with it, comically colliding with his nervous companion and almost falling over. Camilho took to his heels and looked back in time to see the men disappearing into the trees.

During the 1970s witnesses' descriptions of UFO-related entities varied enormously: tall, short, thin, fat, human-like and troll-like beings were reported. By the end of the decade, however, a remarkable synthesis had begun. In North America aliens, especially in cases involving abductions, were almost always described as hairless grey dwarves about 1.2 m (4 feet) tall with large black eyes, negligible ears, nose and mouth set in an over-large pear-shaped head supported on spindly legs. They came to be known as 'Greys' (see plate section).

In the 1980s the wildly assorted beings previously reported were apparently forgotten; American researchers now championed the Greys as proof of visitors from outer space. In previous years sceptics had, quite reasonably, refused to accept the many varied descriptions of extraterrestrials as proof that alien life forms existed because it was inconceivable that Earth was the tourist centre of the galaxy!

While the Greys dominated the United States, the 'aliens' witnessed in Europe were tall and human-like, wore ski-suits and had shoulder-length blond hair. There were variations, of course, but essentially they looked more human than alien. Their characteristics earned them the name 'Nordics'.

During abductions the Nordics were often seen with small robot-like entities who carried out the physical examinations. The Greys and the Nordics sometimes share one characteristic: large eyes. The Iranian entities, although human-like in their proportions, had large black eyes.

Cultural and social trends which originate in the USA are often exported to Britain once they have become established. In the mid-1990s there has been a dramatic increase in the number of reports from Britain featuring Greys. Have the Greys become the dominant extraterrestrial race after an intergalactic power struggle, or is there another explanation? Could social and psychological influences be responsible?

Since 1987 the media have saturated the British public with the Grey image. In that year horror novelist Whitley Strieber promoted his book *Communion*. The face of a Grey featured on its cover and on hoardings advertising the book. People began to be aware of UFO abduction scenarios and of how an alien might appear.

Strieber drew massive criticism from his peers, who accused him of writing a novel in the guise of 'a true story'. The book told of his repeated abductions at the hands of Greys and the detrimental effect these had on his well-being. Strieber followed the book with *Transformation,* which was well above the credibility threshold of even the most gullible ufologists. Yet the book was a sincere attempt to make sense of abduction experiences which seemed essentially dream-like.

Bruised and battered at the hands of his critics, Strieber issued a statement in 1992. He indicated that the source of his experiences lay hidden somewhere on the wilder shores of psychology. In 1996 Strieber published a new book *Breakthrough*, which updated his thoughts on the subject.

Dr Simon Taylor's experience in Iran sent him searching for answers. What he uncovered convinced him that the beings were not extraterrestrials. His journey took him to an expert in Islamic theology called Mustata Chamran. 'His explanation threw a great deal of light on the matter, even though I did not share this man's religious beliefs,' he said. Indeed, Simon described himself as 'a lapsed atheist'.

A political dissident living in Britain had asked Simon to translate some Iranian political writings into English. During the course of the work Simon felt confident enough to mention the subject of UFOs. Simon was surprised when his client agreed with him that the phenomenon was 'real' and added that it had nothing to do with extraterrestrials, but was a deception engineered by the 'jinn'. He steered Simon in the direction of Mustata Chamran for more information. In June 1977 Simon met Chamran in London.

He told me the jinn belong to the 'realm of the unseen', which is a necessary barrier between God and the manifest world. Without this we would perceive the names of God directly, and thus the whole purpose of creation – for this knowledge to evolve through reason and investigation – would not be possible. It would also preclude unbelief, which in Islam, is a necessary 'evil', without which belief would have no meaning.

Islam posits the cosmos as an infinite gallery of signs which point to the existence of God. This 'gallery' is peopled with sentient beings whose responsibility is to investigate the cosmos and come to know and worship God. The unseen realm is also peopled with beings possessed with free will to know and worship – or ignore and reject – their creator.

The jinn are such beings, along with angels. Some of the jinn are believers, some unbelievers. (At this point I began to feel bands of pain tighten around my temples, for I remembered a similar statement from the entities at Ahar.) One of the functions of the unbelieving jinn is to invite man to unbelief. I use the word 'invite' because Chamran pointed out the jinn cannot coerce man into acts of evil, they can only suggest, and leave the choice to man's free will.

I interrupted Chamran to ask whether UFO phenomena could be related to the jinn. He said that UFO 'illusions' were only one way in which the jinn endeavoured to deflect man's attention from belief in God. Since man is always questing for knowledge about his origin and fate, and therefore for the ultimate 'unseen' – God – the UFO illusions, engineered by the jinn, are particularly effective in perverting that quest. Chamran added that UFOs are only one kind of jinn-related manifestation.

Simon then told him about Ahar and Chamran confirmed that he and Reza had encountered the jinn. The next time Simon heard anything of Mustata Chamran was after the Iranian revolution, when he was made Minister of Defence.

There is no doubt in our minds that the outward appearance assumed by extraterrestrials is merely symbolic and culturally appropriate. But is their appearance a product of people's perception, or the work of other forces behind the phenomenon?

When asked about the true nature of the 'visitors' by ufologist Michael Miley, Whitley Strieber replied, 'There is no way to tell. They are what the force of evolution looks like to a conscious mind. Sceptics who maintain that entity encounters are wholly subjective will say that cultural tracking is the result of images being dredged from the subconscious to take starring roles in hallucinations. These images, derived from books, films and cultural beliefs based on science fiction and occult scenarios, are stored in the brain.

Are alien encounters modern folklore? Dr Eddie Bullard is a folklorist at the University of Indiana who has studied almost 800 cases. Bullard concluded:

Abduction reports as a body show far more similarities than acci-dent, random hoaxes or pure fantasies can explain. The consisten-cies in form and content down to numerous minute details demonstrate that abductions make up a coherent phenomenon, whatever its ultimate nature.... If abductions are stories then the accounts should branch off into a different version for each geo-graphical area, but they do not. If abductions are stories the inves-tigator should be able to impose an individual style on them.... The folklorist's wisdom, based on prior experience with folk nar-ratives, denies a purely fantasy or cultural-influence solution for the abduction mystery.

If there are independent, i.e. not wholly psychological, forces behind the phenomenon, the sceptics' view requires modification; it is not witnesses' perceptions which are changing, but the phe-nomenon itself – a single phenomenon adjusting its appearance throughout human history and across cultural barriers. What you see is not what you get.

People have described meeting angels, gods, fairies, demons and extraterrestrials. Strip away the glossy veneer and we might be nearer to revealing what is really behind alien encounter and abduction experiences.

Chapter 6

The Devil in our Midst

During the 1980s and early 1990s a new phenomenon gripped the imagination of the US media and sowed confusion in the minds of the public. Children were claiming to have been abused by members of occult groups. There were also adults who described having been repeatedly abducted since childhood by Satanists who used them in depraved rituals. A new term was born: Satanic Ritual Abuse (SRA).

In the late 1980s the subject was imported into Britain by Church ministers and social workers who had visited the USA and attended conferences organized by extreme Christian groups. There they listened to the victims of SRA, social workers and some police officers who offered evidence of the phenomenon.

On their return to Britain these self-styled experts organized conferences to which social workers were invited and told how to handle cases of ritual abuse. The dam broke and before long the media were bombarding the public with lurid and horrific accounts of torture and sexual abuse perpetrated by a secret network of Satanists who controlled the higher echelons of the police and the judicial system.

As a result, children in Nottingham, Derby, Manchester, Rochdale, Liverpool and the Orkneys were removed from their homes by the social services. Months later the majority of these children were returned to their parents after police investigations had produced no clear evidence to allow prosecutions to go ahead.

What implications are there here for our study of alien abduction? Are those who claim to have been abused by Satanists in the same category as UFO abductees, as some believe?

The book which launched the SRA movement was *Michelle Remembers*, by Michelle Smith (a pseudonym) and her psychiatrist, Dr Lawrence Pazder. This sensational book, first published in 1980, tells the shocking tale of Michelle, a young married woman who comes to Dr Pazder, a pious Roman Catholic, with psychological problems. She unfolds a story of horror that begins when her parents, particularly her mother, turn her over to a group of Satanists in preparation for the advent of the Devil.

Michelle is sexually abused and physically maltreated by the Satanists, who shut her in cages with various frightening animals. The nonsensical climax of the story comes when poor Michelle, undaunted in her faith and resistant to all the Satanists' devilish overtures, witnesses the manifestation of Satan himself. He leads his hooded followers and a group of children in a dance, choreographed like a piece of vaudeville, while chanting a poem detailing his predictions for the next 28 years.

It is significant that the religious rites of these Satanists are an inversion, or mirror-image, of Catholicism in most details. In the story, the Blessed Virgin steps in to rescue little Michelle at the critical moment and Dr Pazder is able to convert the adult Mrs Smith to the Catholic Church. The reader of *Michelle Remembers* will not be too surprised to learn that the pious Dr Pazder left his long-suffering wife and married Mrs Smith, who had left her husband.

This book opened the floodgates in therapy centres all over the USA as young women began to recall Satanic abuse. It could be argued, of course, that the publication of Michelle Smith's story gave other victims confidence to speak out. The thousands of such cases which have since been documented seem to follow a standard pattern. Often the victim is recruited by Satanists and then abused, or is abducted and held prisoner. Sometimes the victim (usually – but not always – female) is brought up in a Satanic family, implying generational involvement.

If the SRA allegations had remained in the therapists' surgeries, they might quickly have been forgotten, but a combination of vocal Christian fundamentalist groups, social workers and even some police officers ensured that the subject was to retain a high profile in the media for several years.

At the height of the SRA allegations, an interesting case fell into the lap of Moyshe Kalman. Zoe Atkins, aged 23, appeared to be a highly intelligent young woman. Her background was working class, both parents being unskilled labourers, but, unusually, the family home was a hotbed of radical politics. Both parents belonged to extreme Communist cells and they taught all their eight children to both fear and hate the established order of society.

For Zoe, to make use of bourgeois private medicine was bad enough, but actually to take seriously the Freudian theory of mind was a total betrayal of practically all her childhood beliefs. However, she was desperate. She had left what she had hoped would be a lifelong career in radical political work under painful circumstances and entered college, hoping to go on to university. Soon after the beginning of her first term at college, Zoe became phobic. She suffered panic attacks which took the form of agoraphobia and had an irrational fear of open spaces and large rooms such as lecture halls. By the time she came to Kalman for therapy, Zoe was having trouble shopping and going out socially and was beginning to feel like a recluse.

Zoe balked at the idea of hypnosis and felt that she was always too much 'in control' ever to succeed with free association – a psychoanalytical method in which the subject is encouraged to allow their thoughts to wander. Although the Freudian theory of repression was totally alien to all that she believed, Zoe did feel as though something in her unconscious was directing her feelings in ways she definitely did *not* want it to. To the surprise of both the therapist and Zoe herself, she not only free-associated without difficulty, but spontaneously went into a trance state which made the whole process much easier. From the first session, Zoe allowed her pent-up emotions to flow and thus her remarkable analysis began.

Psychoanalysis always begins either with a bang or a whimper. Zoe whimpered at first. The early weeks were filled with a frank and objective description of her intense and oppressive childhood and gradually her phobic symptoms began to ease. She felt more and more positive about the analysis. Then a note of concern began to creep into Zoe's voice. Often, at the beginning of a session, she would say something to the effect of: 'I hope I am not going to remember something really terrible about my parents. You don't think I was sexually abused or anything like that, do you?'

Kalman always practises a very strict, non-directed, non-involved therapy, so he never answered Zoe's question nor gave her any indication of what he thought. In fact, he could not detect in her any signs of abuse other than a repression of spirit.

After about two months of therapy and an almost total disappearance of her symptoms, Zoe was very eager to learn more about the underlying unconscious causes of her anxiety, but was increasingly apprehensive about discovering something 'bad' about her childhood that she might not be able to handle emotionally. It was then that her memories of abuse began to surface.

Zoe was as prudish as a good, old-fashioned Communist of the 1930s. To discuss anything of a sexual nature was extremely difficult for her. She believed that Freud was just a dirty-minded old bourgeois. For her, sexuality was associated with middle-class values and had nothing to do with her.

This disassociation with her own sexuality was reflected in Zoe's appearance. She was a stocky woman and she made the worst of her looks by wearing ill-fitting, baggy clothes, having a pudding-basin haircut and sporting very unbecoming glasses. As a child she had been afflicted with very poor vision, which necessitated her attending a special school. While she was separated from her family, her superior intelligence was recognized and she received a very good education.

Zoe had never had a date. Her idea of an exciting social event was spending the evening discussing politics with her gay brother's boyfriend. She sought safety in making herself unattractive and mixing with people who would not threaten her with their attentions.

With great embarrassment Zoe struggled to relate to Kalman a memory about playing in the park as a child. This recollection was in stark contrast to most of her childhood memories, which rarely involved parks, playing or other normal leisure activities. She reverted to childlike speech and could only be persuaded to talk with repeated urgings and promptings and assurances that it was safe and 'all right' to talk.

Suddenly, the dam broke and a rush of memories poured out. Suppressed grief, rage and hurt vied to find expression as Zoe began to tell about a neighbour named Bill. She had known him all her life and did not find it strange when he pulled up in his car as she played and offered to take her for a ride.

Bill took Zoe to a large abandoned warehouse where she saw a room fitted out for 'rituals', complete with altar, inverted cross, chalice and dagger – the usual trappings of Satanic worship. The little girl was afraid and began to struggle and protest, begging pitifully to be taken home. Bill made seductive advances which she did not understand and when it became clear what he wanted of her, she made every effort to repulse him.

Zoe went on to describe a programme of systematic sensory deprivation and brainwashing she suffered, which was very much like that endured by the millionaire's daughter Patty Hearst during her ordeal in California. First Bill locked her in a coffin-like box for hours, if not days, on end. Then he would ritually rape her on the altar, dressed all in black, sometimes in the company of other Satanists. This ordeal was accompanied by ritual chanting, candles, incense and the forced imbibing of foul substances which Zoe claimed were blood and human body products.

As Kalman continued to remain impassive and uninvolved, the infuriated Zoe accused him of leading her on. In fact, before her therapy began, when the concept of repression and the sort of memories that might be reclaimed had been discussed, Zoe herself had brought up the subject of Satanic ritual abuse. She had been reading about it and remarked that she hoped she would not remember anything as terrible as that. Kalman had expressed his doubt that the phenomenon had any basis in fact.

For several weeks Zoe continued to describe her Satanic ordeals, but it began to seem as if she were fulfilling a duty in telling these stories rather than discussing real feelings or memories. The emotion, weeping and accusations started to fade away and Zoe's phobic attacks stopped abruptly when she suddenly remembered that it was she who had first mentioned the idea of Satanism.

Zoe was able to overcome the phobias which had originally driven her to analysis, but she had needed a sensational cause to justify her problems to herself. Assuming that Kalman was a religious person, she must have felt, at least unconsciously, that it was a reasonable plan to invent a myth with religious overtones. Zoe's unconscious mind probably reasoned that this would please Kalman and endear her to him.

Satanic ritual abuse had been publicized around Manchester, where Zoe lived. Reports by supposed experts suggested that Rochdale and Manchester were the European centre for Satanism!

Zoe had opted for the prevailing myth of devil worship. Because she had tried to maintain this belief only within the therapeutic setting and not in the outside world, it never became deeply fixed in her self-image.

Zoe viewed her 'memory' of Satanic abuse more and more objectively and did not feel the need either to convince other people that it had happened or to defend it from attack, and she soon realized that it was inconsistent with what she knew about her childhood – her parents were not aware of any long unexplained absences during which she might have been held captive – nor did it ring true emotionally.

Finally the day came when Zoe had to admit to herself the truth: Bill had always represented an unattainable sexual goal – she had been attracted to him since early childhood.

As a child, Zoe had been made to feel very negative about herself. Her parents constantly drew attention to her poor eyesight and told her that she was not as good-looking as her brothers, and she absorbed this information into her self-image.

Erotic fantasies were taboo for Zoe because she had been taught to think that sex was 'materialistic' and 'bad'; it did not figure in the great workers' paradise dreamed of by her parents. In order to tolerate a taboo fantasy, her longing for Bill, and the desire to love and be loved, Zoe had to make it safe. Like many of the women in Dr Nancy Friday's book, *Women On Top*, Zoe could allow herself an erotic fantasy only if she were the victim. After all, if you are the victim, you are not responsible; it is not your fault, no one can blame you and you just might as well enjoy the experience that is being forced on you.

The nature of her fantasies relieved Zoe of the responsibility of what she felt was the essential 'wrongness' of her normal desires. When she became reconciled to herself and started to appreciate her value as a human being, this defensive structure was no longer needed and it fell away. It left a young woman who began to lead a more productive life, enjoying both her intellectual capacity and the physical reality of her life.

If Zoe had left analysis before its completion, still believing that she had been the victim of ritual abuse, the outcome would have been rather different. There are scores of people, mainly young women, in Britain today who have come out of some form of psychotherapy convinced that they are the victims of Satanism and of a conspiracy to cover up the truth about such abuse. Is there any evidence at all to support such beliefs?

The whole history of Satanism and witchcraft is subject to interpretation and romanticization. Certain New Age groups would have us believe that modern witchcraft is 'the old religion', a pre-Christian paganism which revolved around worship of fertility goddesses and was forced underground in the seventeenth century. On the other hand, right-wing Christian clergy maintain that an organized, deviant and dangerous group of Satan worshippers are plotting to overturn the established order, and the overwhelming verbal evidence of the victims of Satanic abuse supports this theory. There is nothing good and enlightened about these followers of Satan. They are engaged in violent and often fatal sexual abuse, systematic murder of children, abortion, cannibalism, drug-dealing and crime on a large scale.

Historically, both interpretations are valid. The pro-Wicca, Earth Mother followers often describe themselves as 'white witches' or 'wise women', very like herbalists, with a bit of mysticism thrown in. Indeed, there is evidence that many of the unfortunate men and women who were put to death during the widespread witch-hunts of the late Middle Ages were just that: herbalists who also dabbled in love potions, charms against warts and so on. Once the witch craze took hold in Europe and, later, in North America, the concept of witches and sorcery changed dramatically. The idea of the Satanic, demon-raising hag, arising out of Christian theology and superstition, was firmly established in the Renaissance. The prototype for this type of witch does have its roots in antiquity, however.

A first-century writer, Minucius Felix, in his description of the initiation as a witch of a devotee of Hecate, the goddess of witchcraft, states that the process always involved the sacrifice of a young baby, whose blood was ritually drunk and whose limbs were then eaten by the participants. In Renaissance times such stories were organized into a body of 'knowledge' which fitted into the scholastic Christian world-view, thanks mainly to two German Dominican priests, Heinrich Institoris (or Kramer) and Jakob Sprenger, who were appointed by Pope Innocent VIII to write their witch-finder's handbook, the *Malleus Maleficarum*.

There is some evidence that human sacrifice and ritualized child abuse actually happened. In 1678 Nicholas de la Reynie, Louis XIV's Lieutenant-General of Police, discovered a group of upper-class black magic practitioners headed by a Catholic priest called Guignard, whose acolytes included the King's mistress. Central to their rituals was the abuse and sacrifice of young children.

The most striking similarity between the victim of ritual abuse and the victim of extraterrestrial abduction is the problem of retrieving memories. Both types of victim appear to be in a post-traumatic, amnesiac state. The therapist normally becomes involved with the patient before he or she is aware of having been abducted. UFO witnesses remember the *sighting*, but not much else. When therapy opens the gates of memory, the memories, whether accurate or false, reveal a host of similarities.

Alien abductions are followed by forcible and humiliating physical examinations. In the most detailed memories, victims describe painful procedures; often eggs and sperm are taken for use in hybrid-breeding programmes. Alien-induced pregnancies are always terminated in the early stages and the embryo is taken away by the extraterrestrials for further development. In several cases female victims have reported being raped by extraterrestrials and some male abductees have claimed they were forced to have a sexual relationship with seductive female aliens.

In all cases of Satanic ritual abuse sexuality plays a central role. Orgiastic rituals, sometimes mimicking the Mass, are always a main feature. The new recruit or abductee is usually forced to lie on an altar and the Black Mass is celebrated, using the woman's body symbolically in place of the Host and culminating in sexual relations between her and the 'priest'. In almost every case of alien abduction the victim is also placed on a table before the ordeal begins. The UFO abductee is surrounded by aliens, the Satanists' victim sees hooded figures.

Just as some UFO abductees claim that they were made pregnant, only to have the foetus removed before it came to term, a common feature of ritual abuse is the belief that women, often quite young girls, are used by the Satanic circle as 'brood mares'. Victims have described being regularly impregnated to supply either babies or foetuses for sacrifice during the Black Mass.

In both phenomena, implements of a roughly similar nature are involved. The aliens use complex surgical instruments, many of which are intrusive, such as needles and knives. Abductee Whitley Strieber described how one device 'swarmed' up his anus. The Satanic mass involves the use of special ritual knives and daggers and often the abductee describes being tortured with needles and pins.

Both types of victim believe they are 'tagged' so that they can be followed or monitored. Some UFO abductees claim a small electronic device has been concealed in their bodies. Ritual abuse victims describe a vaguer, more mysterious form of surveillance, often a supernatural one; the coven always knows where they are and what they are doing. All victims fear that they can be 'picked up' at any time.

A case which can be considered as particularly persuasive evidence of a link between these phenomena received nationwide publicity in August 1990. A 26-year-old woman claimed that when she was four years old her grandfather had lured her into a coven. Over the next 22 years she was used sexually in rituals and sometimes heard the screams of babies during sacrifice. At the time the story emerged, the woman, known as 'Sarah', was recovering both mentally and physically from her latest ordeal, at Birch Hill Hospital in Rochdale, Lancashire. There, the consultant psychiatrist Dr Victor Harris was treating her.

Harris claimed that an examination of Sarah by a police surgeon confirmed she had been subjected to multiple rape. This assertion was backed up by a journalist, Matt Finnegan, who told Peter Hough he had heard it from a police officer working on the case. However, when Hough contacted the office of the Chief Constable for Greater Manchester, the assertion was denied.

That Sarah believed her story, and that Dr Harris was convinced by it, cannot be denied. He told journalists:

This woman is not crazy or prone to invent things. Her psychological reaction to abuse, torture and experiences beyond the norm are identical to those of victims of the concentration camps. She would have had to do an awful amount of research in psychological textbooks and be an accomplished actress to make it up. She had provided the most mundane details about these rituals and covens, which a liar would not bother with. In my professional judgement she is telling the truth.

Sarah would receive a telephone call and a voice would simply say, 'prepare yourself.' Then a car would arrive and she would be made to lie down during the drive to a secret location. There she would remain for up to four days, subjected to depraved acts on the altar of a Satanist temple.

Despite this her family and friends were unaware of Sarah's double life. Her husband first learned of it when he came across her diary. Like other victims Sarah claims she is unable to name her abusers for fear of retribution. Somehow they know her every move, she believes, and even the movements of her psychiatrist, Dr Harris.

Neither alien abduction nor ritual abuse offer hard forensic proof – only tantalizing and ambiguous evidence. While the UFO phenomenon is more complex, involving radar evidence and multiple sightings, as with Satanic Ritual Abuse, it has yet to be conclusively demonstrated that alien abductions have actually occurred.

In the USA the victims of abuse have shown law officers the alleged location of mass graves, yet to date no bodies have been found. The first victim, Michelle, has not been able to show evidence in any of the places where she claims abuse took place. Nor have the churches and isolated buildings in which ceremonies were said to have been held yielded any evidence. When police officers were tipped off about a supposed ritual or sacrifice they have never found such activities taking place. In a celebrated case in the USA, police arriving to catch a coven at work found a group of men and women in strange robes armed with swords and daggers rehearsing a production of *Julius Caesar* !

Sceptics assert that in alien abduction and satanic abuse only fraud and imagination, sociological forces and multiple personality syndrome are at work. Once one major case grips the public imagination, hundreds more follow. This would seem to point towards mass hysteria as an explanation, but it could just as easily be argued that a well-publicized case gives other victims the confidence to disclose their secrets to a wider world.

Perhaps a better question than 'Did it really happen?' would be 'Why are so many people, with no contact, telling the same type of story?'

There is no doubt in our minds that UFO abductions and the accounts of kidnapping and abuse by anonymous satanists are two aspects of the same phenomenon. For a hundred Zoes who have used the SRA scenario as a psychological convenience, there is one case which seems almost believable – believable enough to convince psychiatrists like Dr Victor Harris.

After the collapse of the Rochdale SRA case Peter Hough spoke to a senior police officer, who commented: 'We never did find any evidence, but the other officers and myself came away with a strong feeling that *something* had happened.'

Chapter 7

It

The following case, more than most, illustrates the different levels on which the abduction phenomenon can operate. The subject, a young woman called Abigail, came to us with a childhood memory of a UFO encounter. Over several hypnosis sessions, much more emerged. We recorded Abigail's recollection, then decided to explore it further using hypnosis. During the first session Abigail went back to being seven years old. This is a transcript of the recording of that session:

KALMAN: *What do you see?*

ABIGAIL: *I'm watching television. Rupert Bear.*

KALMAN: *Is there someone with you?*

ABIGAIL: *My mum. I want to watch television.*

KALMAN: *What's Mummy saying?*

ABIGAIL: *'It's a lovely day, play outside.'*

KALMAN: *What are you feeling?*

ABIGAIL: *I'm a bit annoyed and upset.*

KALMAN: *What's happening?*

ABIGAIL: *Walking outside, I see a ball on the path. I pick it up and take it round to the side of the house, on the driveway. Throwing the ball at the wall.*

KALMAN: *What's happening now? What are you seeing?*

ABIGAIL: *Some kids walk past but I'm not allowed to play with them. They're talking about me.*

KALMAN: *What are they saying?*

ABIGAIL: *They call me a snob.*

KALMAN: *Now tell me what you are remembering.*

ABIGAIL: *I'm trying to play a game but you need two balls, but I've only got one. I'm throwing it in the air and letting it bounce on the ground. I'm looking up to throw it, and something's above me ...*

KALMAN: *What is it? What can you see?*

ABIGAIL: *It's very, very big.*

KALMAN: *What colour is it?*

ABIGAIL: *Grey, it's not moving at all. It's like a dull grey – I can't really believe it. I'm excited, feeling a bit cold.*

KALMAN: *What can you hear?*

ABIGAIL: *I can't hear anything, everything's really quiet. I can't even hear the birds. I'm looking at it again. It's over our roof and next door's too.*

KALMAN: *This is an enormous object.*

ABIGAIL: *It's very big, a bit boring really, there's nothing special about it, it's dull grey and circular – squashed.*

HOUGH: *What do you think it's made of?*

ABIGAIL: *It looks a bit like lead. Metal. Definitely metal but not shiny.*

HOUGH: *Can you see anyone else watching?*

ABIGAIL: *There's nobody else outside.*

HOUGH: *Are you alone?*

ABIGAIL: *Yes.*

KALMAN: *Look around. What else can you see?*

ABIGAIL: *I feel a bit lighter now. The ground's not solid anymore. It feels like I'm hardly touching the floor. I quite like it.*

KALMAN: *Can you hear anything?*

ABIGAIL: *No, I don't think so.*

KALMAN: *What about the bushes – can you see the bushes?*

ABIGAIL: *Yes, the bushes are rustling. I'm a bit worried in case it's the dog next door, because it once bit me.*

KALMAN: *What are you seeing now, what's in the bushes?*

ABIGAIL: *A face looking.*

KALMAN: *Can you see more than a face?*

ABIGAIL: *No, it's just a face, looking.*

KALMAN: *What is this face like?*

ABIGAIL: *It feels like it's smiling at me. It's friendly. I like it – it wants to be my friend. I find it a bit funny.*

KALMAN: *It wants to be your friend?*

ABIGAIL: *Yes, it's quite nice.*

KALMAN: *Are you drawn to it?*

ABIGAIL: *It feels like it's a child, another child. I get the feeling it's a girl. I don't know why. Maybe because it's very, very pale.*

KALMAN: *What about hair, does it have any?*

ABIGAIL: *I can't see any, but I can't see the whole head.*

KALMAN: *Tell me what you can see.*

ABIGAIL: *The forehead down to the chin. The chin's pointed like mine, but a lot longer.*

KALMAN: *And the eyes?*

ABIGAIL: *Very big – different but not horrible. They're dark, and like horses' eyes, with a nice shape to them.*

KALMAN: *The mouth?*

ABIGAIL: *There doesn't seem to be anything there.*

KALMAN: *How is the face smiling at you?*

ABIGAIL: *I just feel it has sent me a smile. The nose is a bit obscure, it's flat.*

KALMAN: *What's happening now?*

ABIGAIL: *I want to touch her to make sure she's really there.*

KALMAN: *Are you getting nearer?*

ABIGAIL: *I put my hand up to try and touch her, but she moves back a little.*

KALMAN: *What do you feel as she moves back?*

ABIGAIL: *I'm disappointed, and I think she knows, so she moves back again and lets me touch her on the face.*

KALMAN: *What does she feel like?*

ABIGAIL: *Quite cold. Thick.*

KALMAN: *What do you see?*

ABIGAIL: *I can hear somebody. It's my mum shouting me. She's saying, 'Come on Bootsy, we're going out now.'*

KALMAN: *You can remember everything that's happening now.*

ABIGAIL: *I'm looking at the house because I can hear her.*

KALMAN: *Look at that face very carefully; tell me exactly what you feel.*

ABIGAIL: *I don't like it any more. She's tilted her head, looking at me, close to me, angry but smiling. The eyes are full of hate. I feel like when I got bullied at school, when someone pretended to be my friend when really they weren't. I'm thinking I'm going to run. I feel like I can't but I know I want to.*

KALMAN: *What's happening now?*

ABIGAIL: *I have to make an effort, I'm thinking really hard. I'm going to do it. I move away and she doesn't like it. She's really angry. I run.*

KALMAN: *What do you see as you rush in?*

ABIGAIL: *All the family are in the kitchen near the door. I said I've just seen a UFO above the house. They laugh so I said come and have a look. No one wants to.*

KALMAN: *Was the face still there?*

ABIGAIL: *No, no. I know about the thing in the sky, but not the other thing in the bushes.*

KALMAN: *When did you forget it?*

ABIGAIL: *As I came into the house.*

KALMAN: *How did you forget it?*

ABIGAIL: *I don't know....*

This is a fascinating account of an experience which must have some basis in reality as it has remained with Abigail for over 20 years. Yet if the UFO really was there, at roof-top height, other people in the neighbourhood should also have been aware of it. It is inconceivable that something like that could have gone un-noticed. This is a dilemma that affects a significant percentage of UFO encounters. There are several possible answers:

1. *The UFO was purely a product of Abigail's imagination.* If that was the case, would it have remained to haunt her into adulthood? Why would a seven-year-old girl fantasize a UFO?

2. *The object was really there, but only Abigail was capable of seeing it.* If UFO phenomena are paranormal, this explanation equates with the claims of so-called psychics who believe that their minds can tune into the 'paranormal highway', allowing them to 'see' apparitions and receive information of which ordinary people are unaware. In Abigail's case, unless passers-by had also been 'psychic' they would not have seen the UFO.

3. *The object was really there, but the forces behind the phenom-enon made sure that only Abigail could see it.* Close-encounter experiences are not accidental or random events, even when they

appear to be. There was a spate of cases during the 1960s and early 1970s when witnesses would 'accidentally' come across a grounded object which had supposedly developed problems with its motive power and was under repair. In retrospect the incidents seem to have been specially staged for the witness in a 'psychodrama' created in order to pass on accurate information and sometimes disinformation.

Many such incidents take place in built-up areas, yet only the victim is aware of what is happening. If hallucination is not the answer, something is controlling witnesses' perceptions and thoughts.

A business man called Mike Sacks was up in the early hours of 24 February 1979 with his wife seeing to his son, who was ill with tonsillitis. Mike lives in the Rossendale valley in North Lancashire, which contains many quarries. Suddenly the bedroom filled with pulsating light and the couple went over to the window. They saw an orange ball travelling at about 160 kph (100 mph). Suddenly it stopped, the glow diminished and a superstructure appeared: three rings which pulsated a deep red colour, bathing the mouth of one of the quarries. Then it sank out of sight.

Mike contacted his brother, who lives about 6.5 km (4 miles) away, and they went to the quarry to investigate. There they met two police officers who had also seen the strange orange ball of light. Carrying torches, the men took the steep path down into the quarry. It was approximately 2.40 am.

There was something in the quarry: an object with a row of lighted windows. All four men walked past, apparently not appreciating how strange it was. Mike found himself unable to look directly at the object and all the while, a voice in his head kept repeating: 'Portakabin . . . Portakabin . . . Portakabin. . .'.

Mike and his brother returned to the quarry in daylight and the building had gone. They had a conversation with the foreman of the gang working there. Mike asked him where they had taken the Portakabin (mobile cabin). The foreman looked bemused and asked, 'What Portakabin?' Mike explained there had been a Portakabin in the quarry the previous night, with its interior lit up. The foreman shook his head and said, 'There's never been a Portakabin. If the lads want a pee they use the Portaloo up there on the ridge.'

It would seem that it was a UFO in the quarry, and the men had walked right past it. Some force had apparently been used to distort their perceptions and make them believe the object they saw was a workmen's cabin. The suggestion was so powerful that Mike never wondered why it should be lit up in the early hours of the morning.

If such a force can operate on this level, might it work on a much grander scale and make whole communities oblivious of its presence? If so, what kind of awesome power might this be?

In further hypnosis sessions with Abigail, another incident involving the entity she had met in the garden emerged. This time she gave it a name, 'Bubby', which indicated that she was familiar with it and led us to wonder whether there were other incidents still hidden from her conscious mind.

When Abigail was 16 she lived alone and personal circumstances drove her to take an overdose of pills. What occurred when she lapsed into unconsciousness could, in another setting, be construed as a near-death experience, or NDE. This reinforces our belief that there is only one core phenomenon from which all manner of paranormal experiences spring. Abigail was regressed to the overdose episode under hypnosis:

ABIGAIL: *I'm in the dark – everything's black. I'm lying on something like water but thick.*

KALMAN: *Is it warm, cold?*

ABIGAIL: *Body temperature, tepid.*

KALMAN: *Can you hear anything?*

ABIGAIL: *A hum.*

KALMAN: *Are you moving?*

ABIGAIL: *Feels like lying on the sea with your eyes closed on a choppy day.*

KALMAN: *Are you rising and falling?*

ABIGAIL: *Yes, my stomach hurts. I can hear someone. Is there someone there? I can't see a thing. This noise is driving me mad!*

HOUGH: *Is it like machinery?*

ABIGAIL: *No. There is somebody around me. I can feel that somebody's there. I feel them but can't see anything. It's like I've got my eyes closed but they're open. I'm feeling a bit panicky. Somebody is telling me to be calm. I can hear them.*

KALMAN: *What does the voice sound like?*

ABIGAIL: *It's not a woman's voice or a man's. It's asking me how I feel. I'd feel better if I knew where I was. It's so dark. Something just touched my hand.*

KALMAN: *What does it feel like?*

ABIGAIL: *Cold, a bit squishy.*

KALMAN: *Hold the hand.*

ABIGAIL: *There's images in my head, I think it's, I think it's the Bubby....*

KALMAN: *Tell me about 'the Bubby'. Can you see it?*

ABIGAIL: *Only in my head. She's not got any bigger.*

KALMAN: *What does Bubby look like?*

ABIGAIL: *Sort of white like a ghost with big horse-shaped eyes, round and very dark. She's nice sometimes, but now she's annoyed with me.*

KALMAN: *What have you done? Why is Bubby annoyed with you?*

ABIGAIL: *Because I tried to waste life. She's telling me I'm very stupid. They want me to do something. I don't know what it is. She says I'll know when the time comes. But how will I know if I don't know? She says so far I've been disappointing. I shouldn't have done it because she's right, life is....*

KALMAN: *What are you remembering now?*

ABIGAIL: *I'm sinking into this stuff. It's all over me.*

KALMAN: *Over your face?*

ABIGAIL: *Yes. God, it's weird. I can breathe in this. I feel a bit like a baby. Stomach pains are going. She's come back.*

KALMAN: *Bubby?*

ABIGAIL: *Yes. she says I've got to go now.*

KALMAN: *Are you going back?*

ABIGAIL: *Yes. I don't know how. I'm a bit sleepy. Floating down, right down. See my room, my bedroom. Floating down. Going to go to sleep.*

HOUGH: *Do you see anything as you're floating down?*

ABIGAIL: *I've got a pink carpet and pink covers with flowers on. White unit with a huge mirror, all my books, red curtains.*

KALMAN: *Tell me what's happening.*

ABIGAIL: *Dreaming. Black things coming to attack me. I've got to get out of bed. I think I'm going to be sick. I can hear someone. There's someone at the door....*

Still under hypnosis, Abigail recalled how a friend had called round because she had not seen Abigail for two days and was concerned. An ambulance was called and Abigail was taken to hospital. During the night she could not sleep because of the noises other patients were making in the ward. Once a woman began to scream and Abigail opened her eyes.

At this point in the session Abigail said she could see Bubby's face above her, smiling. She reported: 'She's telling me I'll be fine. She has to go now and I won't see her for a long time. Many years. She's going.'

When asked how she felt, Abigail replied, 'Like part of me is going away.'

During our work with Abigail we uncovered 'memories' of incidents involving a childhood companion. 'Phantom' companions are generally 'children' of the same age and sex as the percipient. In this instance, however, Abigail's friend was an adult male dwarf. The encounter Abigail recalled under hypnosis began in the bedroom she shared with her infant brother, Sandy.

KALMAN: *Tell me what you're thinking.*

ABIGAIL: *I'm in bed, Sandy's in his cot.*

KALMAN: *What's happening?*

ABIGAIL: *Playing on my bed, trying to wake Sandy.* [Laughs, then sounds surprised.] *There's a door in the wall!*

KALMAN: *Is the door always there?*

ABIGAIL: *No, it's a funny little door.*

KALMAN: *What does it look like? Is it lit up?* [This deliberate attempt to lead the subject fails.]

ABIGAIL: *No, it's part of the wall. I can see a little hand holding onto the door. There's a little someone.*

KALMAN: *What does it look like?*

ABIGAIL: *I suppose he looks like a dwarf. I'm asking if he wants to come and play, and he said 'Yes'. He's climbing up onto the bed and looks a bit like my dad. He's got a beard but he's only little.*

KALMAN: *What's he doing?*

ABIGAIL: *He's picked up a thing. It's got shapes and you have to sort them into different places.*

KALMAN: *Is this a toy?*

ABIGAIL: *Yes, it's mine. He's asking me how to do it. I'm asking if*

> *he wants to play dolls but he doesn't want to. I'm trying to wake Sandy up again.*
>
> KALMAN: *What's the little man doing?*
>
> ABIGAIL: *He's sitting on the bed looking at things. Picking things up and turning them around. He looks at the cars now and the train. I've got a clockwork train. I'm climbing on Sandy's cot but he won't wake up. I'm getting back down and asking him about the door. He says it's always there but I've never seen it before. He asks me if I want to go through it.*
>
> KALMAN: *What are you feeling – what do you say?*
>
> ABIGAIL: *I don't know whether I should or not. I could have a look in it. He goes through and says it's OK. I've stuck my head through and it doesn't look like a wall inside. It looks like a rocky tunnel going through the ground. But my bedroom's up high, so I don't understand. . . . He says he'll come back again and just skips away.*
>
> KALMAN: *Is the door still open?*
>
> ABIGAIL: *Yes, the door's still open, but things seem to be changing. It's like the wall is closing down so I take my head out. I look back at it and it's just a wall. The man was really funny.*

Under hypnosis Abigail described the dwarf as 'old but young, like a small child but grown-up, older' – a familiar description of UFO entities.

It is interesting that during the experience Abigail tried to wake her brother, without success. During bedroom-visitor experiences, whether they involve 'angels', 'ghosts' or 'extraterrestrials', people are usually unable to wake others in the room. Are potential witnesses to a bedroom encounter put into an unnaturally deep sleep?

Abigail did not like her brother very much. Once Sandy would not stop crying, so Abigail undid his reins 'and chucked him down the side of the pram', where his head stuck fast in the spokes. On another occasion she removed her brother from the pram and accidently dropped him down some steps. Her mother smacked her bottom and sent her upstairs to her room. This was a prelude to another encounter with 'the little man' which she recalled in a session with Kalman:

ABIGAIL: *I'm crying. Oh – he's come back!*

KALMAN: *Is his door open?*

ABIGAIL: *He was just there – I didn't see the door open. He's doing a dance on the floor. I'm still crying. I think he's trying to cheer me up. He asks me what I've done, why am I crying?*

KALMAN: *What are you telling him?*

ABIGAIL: *That I dropped Sandy down the stairs.*

KALMAN: *What does he say?*

ABIGAIL: *'He'll be OK, don't worry.' He asks if I want to play but I don't. Then he asks if I want to go in the hole through the wall but I don't want to. I really don't want to.*

KALMAN: *What do you feel when he asks you to go down the hole?*

ABIGAIL: *Curious and scared, but he says there are lots of other children down there for me to play with. I don't know if I believe him or not.*

KALMAN: *Let's move on. What's happening now?*

ABIGAIL: *I'm asking him if he's a gnome. My grandad makes gnomes and he looks like one.*

KALMAN: *What does he say?*

ABIGAIL: *He says he's not a gnome but he doesn't tell me what he is. I'm upset and telling him to go away. He asks why, and I tell him I don't want him here any more. I think he's a bit upset and sad as he walks away with his head down.*

KALMAN: *What do you feel as he sulks away?*

ABIGAIL: *I feel sorry for him. Oh – he's turned around and says, 'If you tell me to go I won't come back again.' I say, 'I don't want you to come back.' ... He goes through the door.*

KALMAN: *Does he close it?*

ABIGAIL: *It doesn't close – the wall magics itself back.*

KALMAN: *What do you see now?*

ABIGAIL: *My mum comes in and asks who I'm talking to. I said, 'The little man in the wall.' She said I can come down now. I ask if Sandy's OK, and she says that, surprisingly, he is. I'm going to Sandy to make sure. I suppose I do like him really, but he's just dead miserable.*

Abigail's encounters tie in nicely with historical accounts of gnomes, elves and fairies attempting to persuade humans to follow them into 'fairyland'. This is another thread in the abduction theme, and in view of Abigail's UFO encounter it is fair to assume that they are connected. What would have happened if she had followed the 'gnome' into the tunnel? He tried to entice Abigail by telling her she would meet other children, just as Pennywise, the clown entity in Stephen King's novel *It*, used colourful balloons to entice his young victims down the storm drain.

Roland, another interviewee, told us that when he was ill as a child and confined to his bedroom, he was visited by a small boy. The boy entered the room from a door that appeared in the wall and played games with him. After several visits the boy tried to persuade Roland to follow him through the door and up a flight of stairs. The sick child declined. He told us he *knew* that if he went through the door he would not return.

If we are dealing with interdimensional beings from alternative realities, what would have happened if Abigail and Roland had gone through the door? Would they have gone in an out-of-body state? Would they be discovered apparently asleep? If he was not to return, as Roland believed, would his mother have found him dead?

The dual motif of the clown – a painted smiling face that is a mask for evil – plays its part in fact as well as fiction, from the Joker in the Batman stories to John Wayne Gacy, the murderer of 33 boys and young men, who worked as Pogo the Clown at children's parties. The clown is the happy smiling face in the car that tries to entice children to take a ride by offering sweets. It has been used to great effect in horror films and books. Yet it also surfaces in the twilight zone of anomalous experience. It is a thread that weaves through the UFO encounter phenomenon.

In the early 1960s Stephanie was ten years old. She lived near St Helens on Merseyside. She and her young friends used to play in aptly named Tickle Avenue, where a row of terraced houses was awaiting demolition. One day they were playing in the gutted buildings when Stephanie and her friend Janice glanced through the broken living-room window of the house second from the end. Something in the room made them gasp. They called over the other children, but they were unable to see what had attracted the girls' attention. Stephanie and Janice could not understand why. Hanging in an alcove, as plain as day, they could see a baggy clown costume (see plate section). They decided to investigate.

Inside, the walls were peeling and debris littered the floor. There was a strong smell of damp plaster and in places the floorboards had rotted. The girls paused in the doorway of the front room.

The room was black with mildew, yet in the midst of all the decay the costume hung like a sparkling jewel a tomato-red satin costume with white spots and frilly cuffs, ankles and collar. Suspended by a loop was a clown's hat with a white pompom sewn on the top. The girls stepped over the threshold into the room. Between them and the alcove was a gaping hole in the floor.

Why were their friends unable to see the costume? They could just touch it if they reached across the hole in the floor. That is exactly what Stephanie decided to do: 'All the while I was conscious of Janice standing behind me. I stretched out my hand, and as I did so, the costume *shimmered*.'

It was like a reflection in a still pond suddenly broken by hundreds of tiny ripples. The girls took to their heels. Many years later, without making any conscious connection, Stephanie began collecting ceramic pierrot dolls dressed in traditional clown costume. The experience apparently did not have an adverse effect on Stephanie, although she does suffer a lot from nosebleeds.

Abigail related the following incident while under hypnosis:

KALMAN: *Tell me what you are remembering.*

ABIGAIL: *We're going to my gran's. I like my gran. She looks after me. She's waiting at the door.*

KALMAN: *Keep talking.*

ABIGAIL: *She's asking me, do I want a piece of cake. Uncle Rodney's here and he's got a box with lots of papers in it. He's looking through it and Gran's shouting.*

KALMAN: *What do you hear?*

ABIGAIL: *She's telling him off for looking in the box. There are things in there which should never come out. She picks it up and throws it on the fire.*

KALMAN: *How do you feel?*

ABIGAIL: *I'm frightened because I've never heard Gran shout before.*

KALMAN: *What's Grandad doing?*

ABIGAIL: *Grandad's not in. I don't like Grandad.*

KALMAN: *Why?*

ABIGAIL: *Grandad's sort of 'funny'.*

KALMAN: *What are you remembering?*

ABIGAIL: *He's scary; he doesn't speak.*

KALMAN: *What can you see him doing?*

ABIGAIL: *I'm going in the back. He has a lot of gnome things. Moulds. I'm putting water in them, messing. He comes out frowning, so I get up and walk away.* [Sighs.] *Go and see my Gran; Grandad doesn't like me. She agrees he doesn't like me; he's a bit funny. She says he scares her too. I remember me and Sandy stayed in the front bedroom. I woke up in the night and there was a face on the wall. It was horrible!*

KALMAN: *How can you see a face in the dark?*

ABIGAIL: *I don't know....*

KALMAN: *Look at the face. What does it look like?*

ABIGAIL: *It's white with very, very blue eyes. Its face is painted, some sort of clown with a big grin. It's horrible; I hate it.*

KALMAN: *Look at that big grin, that painted face. Can you see them clearly?*

ABIGAIL: *Yes.*

KALMAN: *Now tell me what you're remembering, what feelings are coming into your mind.*

ABIGAIL: *I've seen it before.*

KALMAN: *Where?*

ABIGAIL: *At the party – I've seen it at the party. Everybody was there – it was horrible!*

KALMAN: *What's happening?*

ABIGAIL: *Rodney's the blue-eyed boy. Uncle Paul hates him. They're arguing that Grandad always does everything for Rodney and does nothing for Paul. Uncle Paul is big and scary. Squeezes my knee sometimes and it hurts. There's some really loud shouting. Everybody's there: Uncle Max, Auntie Elizabeth – everyone. The kids are scared and I don't know what to do.*

KALMAN: *What are you doing?*

ABIGAIL: *I'm standing next to the fire where the cat is. I can hear Grandad coming downstairs – this is going to be horrible. I'm scared because I know he's going to go mad. He flings open the door and slams it shut. A glass on the fireplace falls on the floor. They're shouting. Rodney pushes Paul. He falls on the glass and cuts his arm. There's blood everywhere. Grandad's just standing there – .... Oh.*

KALMAN: *What do you see?* [Abigail begins to get upset.]

ABIGAIL: *It – the clown's behind him. It's laughing horribly.*
KALMAN: *Describe what you see.*
ABIGAIL: *It's got tights on.*
KALMAN: *What do you feel as you look at those tights?*
ABIGAIL: It's *horrible!* [Begins to cry.] *I can't, I'm sorry. . . .*

Several other members of Abigail's family had strange experiences. For example, one of her uncles dreamed he was on a beach and when he awoke he found a pebble in his hand.

Abigail's mother had a strong influence on her daughter. After the initial encounter with the dwarf, Abigail asked her mother if it was real. She replied that it was possible and that she sometimes saw things other people didn't. When Abigail was ten she pressed her mother with questions about the mind, what it was and how it functioned. Her mother said she would give her a demonstration of what the mind can do. Abigail described the following under hypnosis:

She says she'll show me something to do with the mind. We've got a cigarette lighter, a big glass one. She's putting it on the table and says she's going to move it, but not touch it. Well, that's never going to work! She looks at it. Oh – it's starting to move. . . . I'm going to look under the table; she's doing something. The lighter is moving across the table very slowly.

Abigail asks her mother if she's using trickery and she explains to the child that she too could do it if she wanted.

I don't know what to believe. She tells me that when her headaches were very bad she could make things move in the air. She's talking to me about Egypt too. She's been there but not been there. . . . If I concentrate really hard I can pick up pictures and the noises of people, babble. She tells me she sees lots of things and talks to people – ghosts, because they are not really alive.

Abigail's mother had been blind from birth.

These cases amply illustrate the cross-over between other-world entity encounters. In March 1996 Mark Glover, a paranormal investigator, published the results of a research project carried out for his degree in psychology at the University of Liverpool. It was 'an investigation into the relationship between paranormal, mystical and anomalous experiences; the beliefs and attitudes relating to them and perceptual imaginative factors influencing them'. A hundred and twenty respondents completed a ten-page questionnaire designed by Mark and his tutor.

Two of the main conclusions were that UFO experiences and paranormal experiences are strongly related, but much more so for females than males. Near-death experiences and out-of-body experiences are significantly more strongly related to paranormal experiences than to UFO experiences. Nevertheless, a direct link does exist between NDE and UFO encounters, manifesting in a sort of hybrid experience.

We have already read of Abigail's strange hybrid version of an NDE. Traditionally, people who are dying, or believe they are dying, leave the body and drift down a tunnel towards a bright light. Sometimes they are accompanied by an entity. When they reach the light they are told that their time has not yet come, so they must go. At this point they return to their bodies at tremendous speed.

In Chapter 3 we heard how Janet went down a tunnel during one of her abductions. Abductees often find themselves in a room that is brightly lit without any obvious source of lighting. Here is an experience related to us by Laura Bond, who will feature later in the book:

I was lying in bed one morning feeling very tired after a bad night with my baby and complaining to my husband, who suggested I should lie in. Wide awake, suddenly I felt myself being sucked up into the air at great speed. Below, I could see myself lying in bed with my baby and husband next to me. Suddenly I had a terrible feeling I was going to die. Using all my 'energy' I managed to come back down. It was an inner energy I didn't know I had. I leaped out of bed and refused to get back in again.

On another occasion Laura described being pulled downwards into a tunnel of light.

Professor Kenneth Ring, a psychologist at the University of Connecticut, is a leading researcher into NDEs. His statistical analysis of NDE and UFO abduction accounts demonstrated that they were linked. He confirmed what many researchers already suspected: most of the people who have such experiences are visually creative. Based on this research, Ring wrote a book called *The Omega Project* in which he put forward his theories and conclusions.

Kenneth Ring postulates that other-world experiences are neither 'reality' nor 'fantasy' as we understand the concepts. He thinks that such experiences take place in another realm, which he calls 'the imaginal'. There, the powers of the mind are released, rendering our imaginary experiences real. Ring regards the apparent increase in paranormal experiences as proof of an evolutionary leap in consciousness.

Chapter 8

The Invasion of Black Brook Farm

Black Brook Farm is situated on the edge of a village surrounded by flat Lincolnshire countryside. The farmhouse is almost 200 years old. Along the edge of the property is an abandoned railway embankment. In early 1979 an event occurred that left an indelible blot on the owners' lives.

Mr Bond worked as an accountant and was often late arriving home. One evening, his wife Joyce and his daughters were watching television. The girls, Jayne, Laura and Susan, were aged fourteen, twelve and ten respectively. That evening it was cold and dry, with a bright moon and stars in a clear sky. Thirteen years later, when they first told us their story, the women thought the incident happened on a Monday or Wednesday night, because at the time they were preparing to watch the television soap *Coronation Street*.

Jayne told us: 'Although we're unsure of the exact date, the incident is very clear in our minds even after all this time.'

As the music of the opening credits sounded, the telephone rang. The caller was Sandra Steech, a schoolfriend of Jayne's who lived on a pig farm about 400 metres ($^1/_4$ mile) away. Sandra had called to say that she and her mother had been observing a row of lights hovering over the railway embankment. They had been alerted by their dogs barking. Strangely, the Bond's dog Jason had not reacted at all.

During the half-hour of the Steechs' observation, Sandra said the lights had moved silently and slowly, circling Black Brook Farm. In a statement, Sandra commented: 'Mum and I watched from the sitting-room window, not knowing what it was. I'm sure we would have heard an aircraft at such close quarters.'

Sandra and Jayne kept in contact during much of the subsequent experience. According to Mrs Steech, at one stage Jayne told Sandra that an object was landing, although none of the Bonds remember this. Nor do they remember at what point they broke communication with the other farm. No one thought of calling the police, as they did not believe the authorities could do anything.

Mrs Bond and her daughters looked out of their window and noted a red light 'about the size of a car' rising and falling, gliding about 2 metres (2 yd) above a field across the lane. The movement did not seem erratic, but methodical. When Jayne told her friend they could see the object across the field, Sandra insisted that it was directly over the house. They were obviously observing two different phenomena. The girls followed their mother to the front door. Sure enough, a huge object was hovering just a few metres above the roof of their stable building. Joyce Bond relived that moment for us:

I opened the front door and saw it. I said, 'There it is!' and pulled my youngest daughter back by the collar. To say we were terrified is an understatement. Nothing before or since has had this effect on me. I was shaking all over like a leaf. I'm not usually the sort to panic.

Laura's memories of that night match those of her mother and sisters:

It was 7.30 pm and I was watching television when the phone rang. It was my sister's friend from the pig farm. The next thing I remember is standing in the front doorway with my mum and two sisters, staring at the object. It was very large, almost as big as our house, hovering just feet above the stable opposite. It was just a mass of red and orange lights, and was totally silent. I felt it was watching us.

The object was so brightly lit that it was hard to determine its exact shape. It was illuminated by a mass of dazzling 'electric' lights which flashed alternately. What alarmed the family was the closeness of the object and its total silence.

'Suddenly Mum grabbed my younger sister and we ran indoors,' Laura said. 'I was shaking and closed the curtains. We thought the house was going to catch fire.'

They stood trembling by the phone. Jayne suggested they turn off the television and all the lights. Mrs Bond locked the door.

The measure of their fear was expressed by Jayne's behaviour. In blind panic, she attempted to leave the house by climbing out of a small high window at the back. Her fear cut through to a basic and primitive response: she wanted to run away from the thing and hide under a bush. The others pulled her back. Jayne explained:

We were plain terrified. We thought it would land on the house and kill us. We ran around shaking from head to foot. Such fear stops you from doing anything rational. None of us can remember much after we saw it over the stable.

Mrs Bond then rang her husband at work and told him to come home at once. Jayne told us they tried to escape through the front door to a neighbour's house:

We all ran out again with the purpose of going next door for help. But we tried to take a short cut over the muck heap and couldn't get there, so we all ran back inside. I don't remember where the craft was at that time; I don't remember even looking for it.

After all the toing and froing Joyce Bond was very shaken. It was Jayne who decided to telephone their neighbour, who lived just 200 metres (200 yd) away. By the time he came over the object had moved from over the stable. The Bonds recall standing at the front gate with him and watching the red object across the field until it disappeared behind some trees. Laura said:

I remember us all running outside and seeing an object across the road. I don't think it was the same as the first; it had red lights only, and was smaller. It glided slowly and in a wave-like motion, silent and with purpose.

Finally, the larger object made an appearance, heading in a south-easterly direction over the railway embankment. Laura and Susan remember that a smouldering bonfire lit earlier in the day flared into flame 'in a flash' as the object passed over it and disappeared from sight. They stayed out for some time after that, observing a number of low-flying aircraft from RAF Finningley. Jayne remarked that there seemed to be a lot of military activity:

We live just a few miles from RAF Finningley, and that night there were a lot of little red lights. We presumed they were planes from Finningley looking for the UFOs. They are not usually out in such numbers after dark. I saw them over near Haxey, and Mum remembers them near Santoft.

When Mr Bond arrived home he described how a police road-block had stopped him taking the usual road into the village. The officers told him there had been an accident, although he could see no evidence of one. Neither was he aware of any report subsequently appearing in the local newspapers. As he drew near to the farm by a different route, Mr Bond noticed the top of a fence post on fire.

Later, Jayne learned that a friend living about 3 km (2 miles) away in the next village had observed a bright-red object travelling straight upwards into the sky at around 9 pm. Joyce Bond spoke to Jack Osborne, who owns a smallholding further down the road. He recounted how he too had seen the object, along with his daughter, who clung to him in terror.

In 1994 it was agreed that we should attempt to explore the events of that night using hypnosis. Joyce Bond and her daughters felt that their recollections were somehow incomplete. With varying degrees of eagerness, the women wished to find out whether anything other than what they remembered had happened.

One session each was carried out with Joyce and Susan. Laura was too afraid to take part. These sessions were not very successful, owing to the women's nervousness and underlying fear of what might emerge. Jayne, however, wanted to know the truth, regardless of the consequences. What emerged in the initial session with Jayne were details missing from her conscious recollection of the event:

KALMAN: *What are you remembering, Jayne?*
JAYNE: *I'm scared. There's a bright light. Is there a light on in here?*
    [Regressed subjects are in two places at once, 'here' and 'back there'.] *Are you shining a light in my eyes?*

KALMAN: *No, you're remembering a light. What's happening?*

JAYNE: *Going all black. I can't see anything.*

KALMAN: *Let yourself go forwards to a memory.*

JAYNE: *There's a white light. A door there. I don't know what I'm so scared of ....*

KALMAN: *Where are your memories taking you? Back to that night?*

JAYNE: *No!*

KALMAN: *Yes, we're going back to that memory of the light. You know what you need to remember ....*

JAYNE: *Oh, my hands!*

KALMAN: *What about them?*

JAYNE: *Tingling. My fingers. I'm shaking. All I can remember is standing in the lounge. Don't know why I'm shaking.*

KALMAN: *Tell me why you're so frightened.*

JAYNE: *I don't want to go. I'm scared. I want to run away. There's something there. Something white.*

KALMAN: *Tell me what you are thinking.*

JAYNE: *I don't feel hypnotized. I'm supposed to see it and I can't.*

KALMAN: *But you feel it, don't you?* [Jayne begins to cry.] *You feel the fear. Just relax and let the fear take you into a memory. Say anything that comes into your mind.*

JAYNE: *This is stupid!* [Continues crying.] *My teeth won't stop chattering. Frightened.*

KALMAN: *Were you frightened that night? Were your teeth chattering?*

JAYNE: *Yes.*

KALMAN: *Was the light shining in your eyes?* [Jayne becomes upset again and Kalman calms her down.] *Who's with you?*

JAYNE: *Susan. She's sitting by the fire, watching telly, I think. Don't know where everyone else is, though.*

KALMAN: *Where's Mummy? Did the phone ring? Can you hear it? I think it's for you.*

JAYNE: *Hello, Sandra.*

KALMAN: *It's Sandra. What are you thinking?*

JAYNE: *I can't see anything. It's horrible.*

KALMAN: *What's so horrible, Jayne?*

JAYNE: *The white. I'm at the lounge door and I'm very frightened. There's a white light. I can't bear to look.*

KALMAN: *Keep talking.*

JAYNE: *Standing by the phone. All very frightened.*

KALMAN: *Is the white light in the house?*

JAYNE: *No, it's behind the door! Look out of the window. No ... no .
.. no ....* [Becomes agitated.]

KALMAN: *What do you see out of the window?*

JAYNE: *No, don't ... don't ... don't ... don't ... don't! No! No! No!
Must get out of the window. Mum ... Mum ... Mum .... Light's
gone now.*

HOUGH: *Jayne ....* [The mention of her name shocks Jayne out of
hypnosis and she sits up. Afterwards, Jayne explained that the
way Peter Hough spoke her name reminded her of another,
unspecified, time when 'something dreadful' had whispered
'Jayne' into her ear. Kalman gets her to relax and she is taken
back to the time immediately after the telephone call.]

JAYNE: *Mum's coming. Look out of the window. It's over the road.
What is it? Look outside. It's over the stable. It's big. I can see
it clearly now. I see big lights, red and yellow.*

KALMAN: *Close your eyes and remember.*

JAYNE: *No!*

KALMAN: *What is it? What did you just remember?*

JAYNE: *Big, big, big, round. Frightened. Very frightened.* [She is getting very upset.]

HOUGH: *Relax, Jayne. It's only a memory. It can't hurt you.*

JAYNE: *It's round, big, round, flashing, like a big, big ball.*

HOUGH: *What's happening now?*

JAYNE: *We're looking at it. We're just standing there, looking at it.
Not doing anything.*

KALMAN: *What are you feeling?*

JAYNE: *I'm not feeling anything. I don't know why I'm frightened. I
should never have been frightened.*

HOUGH: *Is it making any noise?*

JAYNE: *No.*

At this point Jayne began to emerge from hypnosis again and
Kalman got her to relax. She asked for the lights to be turned down
and we sat in subdued light. Jayne explained that 'back there' white
light was shining into her eyes. Then, with some difficulty, she was
persuaded to return to the farm and her recollection continued:

The late Professor J. Allen Hynek (centre) created the classification system which includes the now-familiar term 'close encounters of the third kind'; see Introduction. (Peter Hough)

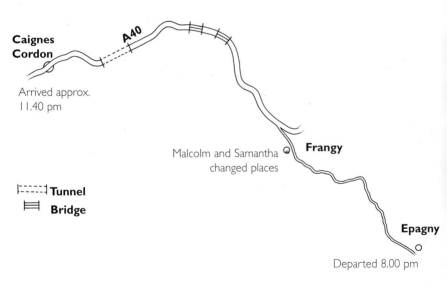

Caignes Cordon

A40

Arrived approx.
11.40 pm

Malcolm and Samantha
changed places

Frangy

⌐┄┄┐ **Tunnel**
┠───┨ **Bridge**

Epagny

Departed 8.00 pm

Map showing the route of Malcolm and Samantha's journey between Epagny and Caignes Cordon. It took them three and a half hours to cover 65 km (40 miles); see Chapter 2.

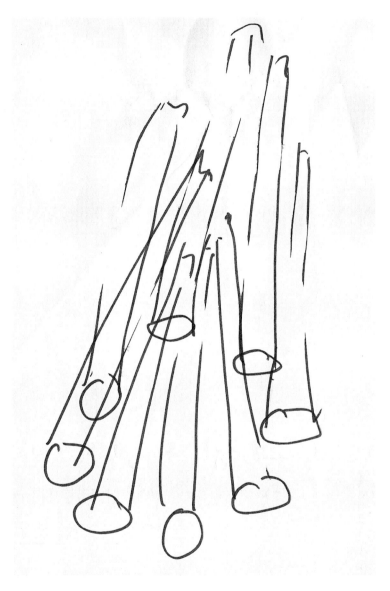

Above: *Malcolm's sketch of the eight beams of light that ended abruptly in mid-air, as if they were solid; see Chapter 2.*

Right: *Samantha's sketch of an image which flashed into her mind after the UFO encounter, with figures to give an idea of scale; see Chapter 2.*

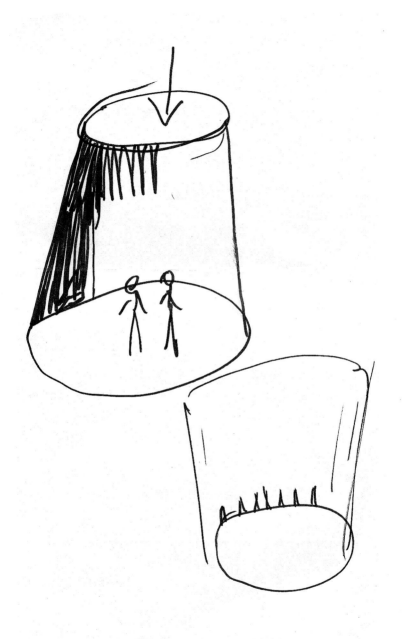

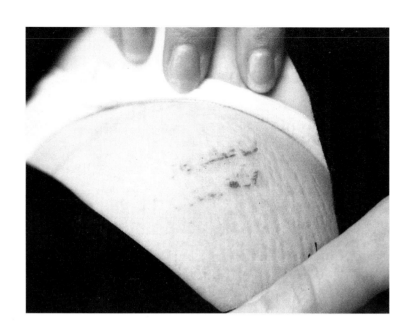

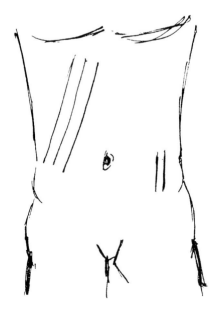

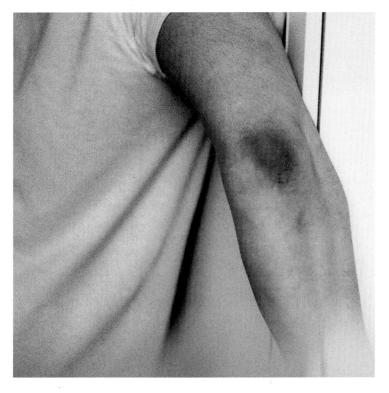

Above: *One of the injuries Stephen Pal inexplicably sustained after dreaming of being taken away; see Chapter 3.* (Peter Hough)

Opposite top: *Abigail cannot explain these painful marks, which appeared on her left hip in the early hours of 17 April 1996, two days before this photograph was taken; see Chapter 3.* (Peter Hough)

Opposite bottom: *Stephen Pal's sketch of the strange injuries he obtained in the night. The shorter scratches are about 8 cm (3 in) long, with a gap of about 2 cm (less than 1 in) between them; see Chapter 3.*

Above: *Detail from the photograph of the mysterious figure Philip Spencer claims he saw on Ilkley Moor in December 1987; see Chapter 4.* (Peter Hough)

Opposite top: *Geoffrey Crawley's attempt to computer-enhance the photograph of the Ilkley 'alien'; see Chapter 4.* (Peter Hough)

Opposite bottom: *Peter Hough (far right), at the scene of the Ilkley abduction, explaining the story to a Granada Television crew; see Chapter 4.* (Vicki Newcombe)

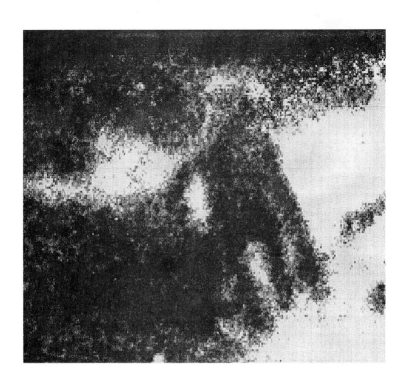

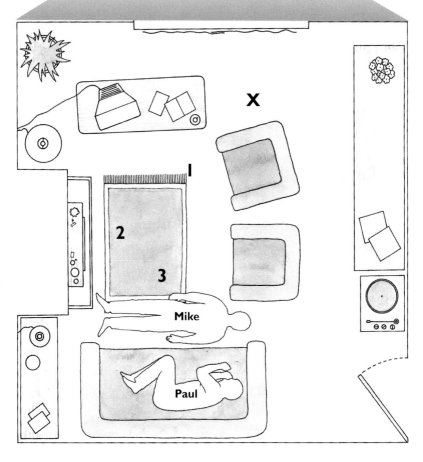

**sodium streetlamp,
10 m (30 ft) away, very faint through curtains**

X

Mike

Paul

X *Where it appeared and disappeared from Paul's line of sight*

3 *It was leaning down and looking at Mike on the floor when
it appeared to notice Paul and turned away*

2 *It looked back at Paul while moving away*

1 *It seemed to stop momentarily and look back again for a bit
longer before again disappearing behind the armchair and out
of Paul's sight*

Above: *Paul's drawing of the 'ugly being' he saw; see Chapter 5.*

Opposite: *Based on an original drawing by Paul, this diagram shows the layout of the living room where he encountered the small 'ugly being'; see Chapter 5.*

*A science-fiction illustration from the 1930s depicting invaders
unlike any described by present-day UFO percipients;
see Chapter 5.*

Artist's impression of the commonly reported type of alien known as a 'Grey'; see Chapter 5. (James Shaw)

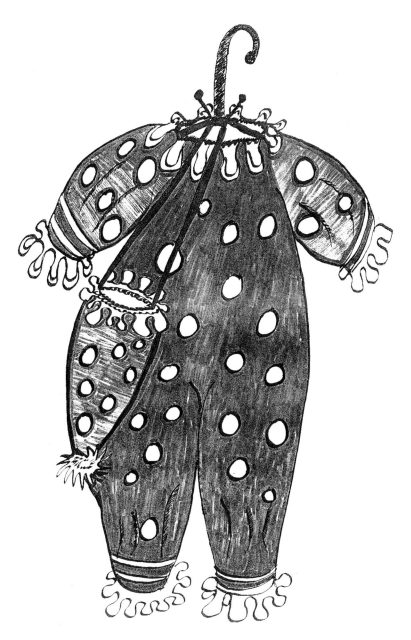

The clown – a figure of jollity – also has a sinister side and has cropped up in abduction accounts. This is a drawing by Stephanie of a costume she and her friend saw in a derelict house; see Chapter 7. (Peter Hough)

The location of Shelley's UFO sighting, with an impression of the object she saw. The houses in the background had not been built at the time of the encounter; see Chapter 8. (Peter Hough)

Jayne Bond's drawing of an image that flashed into her mind during a hypnosis session. The object was larger than a car, but smaller than a bus, and had shining lights; see Chapter 8.

Above: *The leading abduction researcher Budd Hopkins, who believes that extraterrestrials are using humans for genetic experimentation; see Chapter 10.* (Peter Hough)

Opposite top: *The corrugated-iron roof of the Bonds' shed, which was lifted up and turned over, although a nearby heap of straw and a halter hanging on a nail were undisturbed; see Chapter 10.* (Peter Hough)

Opposite bottom: *The bedroom at Black Brook Farm where Jayne Bond was frequently paralysed and confronted by an incubus-like entity; see Chapter 10.* (Peter Hough)

Left: *Betty and Barney Hill, who claimed to have been abducted on 19 September 1961; see Chapter 14.* (Reeves Studios)

Right: *The horror writer Whitley Streiber, who believes he has been abducted by aliens; see Chapter 15.* (Peter Hough)

JAYNE: *Orange. All orange. Everywhere. Not the stable, at the back. Like a sunset. All orange, like the sun's crashed.*

KALMAN: *What are you doing?*

JAYNE: *I'm shaking. Can't stop shaking.*

HOUGH: *What does the orange ball do?*

JAYNE: *Nothing. Looking at us. Go away!*

KALMAN: *What's looking at you, Jayne?*

JAYNE: *Red, orange ball.*

KALMAN: *How can a ball look at you?*

JAYNE: *It's just hovering. Better not look at it. We're going in, shutting the door. Oh God, I want to get out of the window. How stupid! Got to get out of the window. Got to run, run, run away. Hide under a bush, under a bush. 'Cos it's all white .... Susan's there, Mum's there, Laura's there. All there – frightened. Shut the curtains. We can hide, hide, hide. It can't see us now.*

Jayne had realized that the red light they had seen across the field was not the same one that had hovered above the stables. The next memory she recalled involved the smaller red object.

JAYNE: *I'm standing in the yard. That can't be right. I can see the red one. No, it never came that close. Couldn't have done. Couldn't ....*

HOUGH: *What's it doing, Jayne?*

JAYNE: *Big red thing. Next to me. No, no, no!*

KALMAN: *Are you near it?*

JAYNE: *Yes. It didn't happen.*

HOUGH: *Can you describe it?*

JAYNE: *It didn't happen.*

KALMAN: *It doesn't matter. Tell us your fantasies.*

JAYNE: *It's a big red thing coming right by the gate. I'm in the yard. It's coming. Big red balloon. No, it's not true, it's a dream! It's going by the gate, like a big...honey-pot ant.*

KALMAN: *Honey-pot ant?*

JAYNE: *Yes. The big bit with the honey in. Red without the legs. This is ridiculous, because it did not happen .... What's that over there? I have a horrible feeling there's something behind me, by the bank.* [She begins to emerge from hypnosis.]

KALMAN: *Close your eyes.*

JAYNE: *I'm not hypnotized.*

KALMAN: *No, of course not. Tell me what you're remembering now.*

JAYNE: *Sitting down by the muck heap. It's behind me. Look, it doesn't happen like this. I'm sitting by the muck heap – probably in it. Where are the others? Must be a dream. Big red thing's going past the gate and there's something behind the bank. None of this happened.*

KALMAN: *It's OK, Jayne. You tell us what you're imagining.*

JAYNE: *Imagining? There's something behind. I don't want to look. Why am I sitting on the muck heap? Why am I on my own?*

KALMAN: *Does the muck heap smell?*

JAYNE: *Yes.*

KALMAN: *All soft and messy. What are you remembering now?*

JAYNE: *I feel very upset.* [Her voice begins to tremble.]

HOUGH: *Why?*

JAYNE: *This is going to sound stupid. I've been dropped in the muck heap.*

KALMAN: *How did you drop into it?*

JAYNE: *Like that!* [Laughs.] *This is so stupid. It didn't happen like this. We ran over the muck heap and back. We went out with John* [the Bonds' neighbour] *and looked at it. I didn't sit on the muck heap and I wasn't on my own, and it didn't go by the gate. It's just my mind. Why do I keep shaking? Why am I so scared? Why?*

KALMAN: *You're remembering something. Let your mind take you to a memory, Jayne. You're almost there. Tell me what you're seeing. Close your eyes.*

JAYNE: *I'm in the lounge again. Mum's there, Laura's there. We're going to make a run for it. Shut the door. I'm going round and round and round. Where am I going? Don't want to go. I feel I'm going round and round.*

KALMAN: *Is the house going round?*

JAYNE: *Me.*

HOUGH: *What do you see?*

JAYNE: *Orange. I'm not going round now. In the lounge again. We didn't make it.*

HOUGH: *Didn't make it where?*

JAYNE: *To John's house. Couldn't get over the fence; the muck heap's in the way. Ran back again. Oh dear! I don't want it to land on my head. Very near. I'm ducking my head down.*

KALMAN: *Can you hear anything?*

JAYNE: *Can't hear it, can't see it. I'm walking with my head down.*

KALMAN: *How do you know it's there, Jayne?*

JAYNE: *Because there's pressure. Pushing on my head because it's so close. This isn't right because it wasn't there ....*

HOUGH: *Just tell us what you think.*

JAYNE: *Well, it's just a story, Peter. Going out to John's house and there's a big black thing over my head. It's pushing my head down. It's not right. I've got a headache. Over my head. Oh dear, my neck.*

HOUGH: *What's happening to it?*

JAYNE: *It's a dream, it didn't happen. All right ... I see this big flat black thing. It's black and there's something under it. It's square. It's just a dream. Not really happening, because I wasn't on my own, I didn't go out on my own. Wouldn't have done ....*

Through hypnosis, several buried memories were added to Jayne's conscious recollections. She is constantly fighting against these memories, telling herself and the investigators, 'It never happened,' it was only a dream, a fantasy. It would seem that something she was not aware of did happen during the aborted flight over the muck heap. Where were her mother and sisters at the time? Is this new version a fantasy? Jayne feels that if anything more than she consciously remembers did happen, it occurred in the lounge.

The implication is that, during the flight over the muck heap, Jayne – and possibly her mother and sisters too – was abducted. The smaller red object, which she previously remembered remaining in the distance, came right up to her. The image of the 'big red thing' is reminiscent of the huge balloons that chase after Patrick Mac-Goohan in the cult television series, *The Prisoner*.

During regression Jayne believed that she was sitting in the muck heap because that is where she was dropped, presumably from one of the hovering objects. Interestingly, the pressure she felt matches the experiences of many other close-encounter subjects. Philip Spencer also described a pressure bearing down on him and so did Shelley, a young woman interviewed by Peter Hough in 1986.

At 17 Shelley was confronted with a disc-shaped UFO near Bolton in Lancashire on 23 January 1976 while she was on her way home after work (see plate section). Shelley told Peter:

Suddenly it tilted towards me, then there was a terrible pressure on my head and shoulders, and an off taste in my mouth. My teeth seemed to vibrate. When I tried to run it was like being in a nightmare. My arms and legs moved in slow motion. I tried to scream but nothing came out. Then everything went hazy until I remember bursting through the door at home.

Shelley discovered that a ten-minute walk from the bus stop had taken three-quarters of an hour. The fillings in her upper teeth had fallen out, and the bottom ones had turned to powder.

Jayne's hypnosis testimony may have been a fantasy, but it is extremely unlikely that she could have known about the sensation of pressure reported by other subjects, even if she was well-read in UFO literature.

There were several things in Jayne's testimony under hypnosis that did not fit in with her conscious memory of that night at the farm. The first was the blackness followed by a white light she referred to. As we know from other cases, blackness is a prelude to emerging in the white light of the examination room. Jayne is always on the edge of a breakthrough, but her fear keeps the door on her scariest memories firmly shut. In another session the white light returns to dominate her thoughts. At one point, still hypnotized, she opens her eyes to see us standing over her, which she finds very disturbing:

HOUGH: *Why did it frighten you, us standing there? Did it remind you of something?*

JAYNE: *White, white, in the lounge. The white.*

HOUGH: *What's white?*

JAYNE: *Bright white light.*

KALMAN: *Shining through the window, the door?*

JAYNE: *No, in the lounge. I'm scared. I'm standing looking at the wall and so is Mum, and I can see white but I don't know why.*

HOUGH: *Before, you mentioned a blackness. Do you remember?*

JAYNE: *Susan kneeling by the fire. I'm looking at her.*

KALMAN: *What happened before Susan knelt by the fire?*

JAYNE: *No! No!*

KALMAN: *You can tell me about it.*

JAYNE: *Can't! My head hurts!* [She is agitated and opens her eyes again.]

KALMAN: *Close your eyes. What happened before Susan knelt by the fire?*

JAYNE: *All black. Can't remember. Don't know.*

KALMAN: *You can remember it. What happened before Susan knelt?*

JAYNE: *No!* [She becomes hysterical and spontaneously emerges from hypnosis.]

During a later session Jayne's thoughts automatically return to the lounge at Black Brook Farm on that night. Something is troubling her greatly:

JAYNE: *Oh, my head! I feel giddy. My hands have gone tingly. My head feels really weird. I can see orange. Don't like the hall door.*

KALMAN: *Is that door open?*

JAYNE: *No, don't want it open. Door's shut! Shut! Glass door.*

KALMAN: *Can you see through the glass?*

JAYNE: *Funny colour. Sort of blue. Weird, feel floaty.*

KALMAN: *Remember everything that's happened to you as you float.*

JAYNE: *No.*

KALMAN: *Did someone tell you not to remember?*

JAYNE: *No, no!*

KALMAN: *Are you sure?*

JAYNE: *Don't know .... Frightened.*

KALMAN: *Frightened of what?*

JAYNE: *There's something there, that's why I'm frightened.*

KALMAN: *Let's go see what it is, Jayne.*

JAYNE: *I feel like I'm on rollers. I'm going somewhere but I'm not walking.*

KALMAN: *Where are you being taken?*

JAYNE: *Door. I'm going through the door. Tingly. It's going up my arms and in my feet. They're not taking me anywhere! I'm stuck in the lounge feeling weird. I'll be stuck by the settee forever. Think my feet are going now.* [Yawns.]

KALMAN: *Are you feeling sleepy?*

JAYNE: *Just feel weird. Can't see a picture but can see a colour. It's a whitish blue. Pins and needles in my hands. Feel faint. There's a weird light. Violet.*

Jayne's account moves to the point where the family go outside and see the light above the stable. It appears that she – and, by implication, her mother and sisters also – is in a state of altered consciousness.

KALMAN: *What do you feel as you look at it?*

JAYNE: *Dopey. I've got my head on one side. I'm looking up. I'm dopey.*

KALMAN: *Why are you staying there, because you are dopey?*

JAYNE: *Yes.*

KALMAN: *Is Laura dopey?*

JAYNE: *Yes – everybody's dopey.*

KALMAN: *What's happening now? You can remember everything. Isn't it marvellous? Remember everything ....*

JAYNE: *Can't, though. Hypnotize my head. Make me ....*

KALMAN: *Has the dopeyness gone?*

JAYNE: *Yes.*

It would seem that something was happening even before the warning call from Sandra Steech. There is some confusion as to how many objects there actually were. Jayne's next hypnosis session, which begins with her father's return, clarifies this point:

JAYNE: *Now Dad's back. I don't know why, but we go down the road to look for it, which is stupid, because it went the other way.*

KALMAN: *In the car? What did you see?*

JAYNE: *Me and Dad, we didn't find it, we couldn't because we went the wrong way. We went for an hour the wrong way!*

KALMAN: *Why did you go the wrong way? There's a reason – what is it?*

JAYNE: *Mustn't.*

KALMAN: *Mustn't what?*

JAYNE: *See it.*

KALMAN: *Why mustn't you, Jayne?* [She starts to cry.] *You can tell me. Why mustn't you go and see it?*

JAYNE: *It's not right. It's not an aeroplane.*

KALMAN: *Who told you it's not right? Just once you can tell me.*

JAYNE: *Mustn't, mustn't, mustn't look at it ....*

KALMAN: *Tell me why you mustn't.*

JAYNE: *Because it looked at us. It was watching us.*

KALMAN: *What was watching?*

JAYNE: *Could see through the walls. The ball.*

KALMAN: *A ball can watch you, a ball can see you? What was seeing you? What was watching you?*

JAYNE: *You want me to say what it was but I don't know what it was.* [Jayne remembers seeing the big object near the pig farm.] *It's in the wrong place, it shouldn't be there.*

HOUGH: *What do you mean 'It's in the wrong place'?*

JAYNE: *It's near the pig farm and it ... the lights are like diamonds. Not flashing. In the back paddock, like a big ....*

KALMAN: *Big what?*

JAYNE: *Something to do with a clown. Diamonds. Wow, it's flat on top and angled at the side. Flat on the bottom with a round thing on the top. It's all angular and these lights are red and yellow. Oh, this is stupid! It's flat on top and flat on the bottom and there's a little clear bit on top. It's over the field. I never saw it, but it's there and I'm in the yard looking at it, but it doesn't make sense because I never saw it there ....*

HOUGH: *Could it be the same object?*

JAYNE: *It's the same one, oh yes, yes! I can see it now because it's not so close and it's not flashing. It's just lit up.*

In a later session Jayne describes the black object again: 'Like a flat black thing. I think there's stars on it. Looks like a sky with stars. I think it was trying to look like the sky.'

There are real indications that Jayne is holding back on telling us about a full-fledged abduction experience. When she recounted a story about her father cutting down a tree which fell across the drive, leaving them trapped, Kalman used this concept to explore the events that took place at Black Brook Farm:

KALMAN: *Tree's fallen across the drive – trapped. What does 'trapped' remind you of?*

JAYNE: *Dark.*

KALMAN: *Tell me about the dark.*

JAYNE: *Forget. Why am I saying that?*

KALMAN: *Is someone telling you to forget?*

JAYNE: *No.*

KALMAN: *I believe they are. Are you going to obey them? Tell me what you see.*

JAYNE: *I want to forget.*

KALMAN: *What's in your mind that you've never told anybody?*

JAYNE: *Nothing. Total blackness.*

KALMAN: *Imagine yourself merging into the blackness.*

At this suggestion, Jayne becomes hysterical and starts to scream, but after a while she is persuaded to continue:

JAYNE: *Oh no! Get off me! Don't touch me! Get them off me!*

KALMAN: *Who's there on you?*

JAYNE: *Get it off me! Get it off me! Get it away from me!*

KALMAN: *Tell me what you're seeing. Talk about it as much as possible. What's happening to you?*

JAYNE: *Were you touching me?*

KALMAN: *What's happening?*

JAYNE: *Horrible. Get it away. Don't, don't touch me. Forget. Good .... I feel like I'm in the air.*

KALMAN: *Are you very high in the air, looking down?*

JAYNE: *Think so.*

KALMAN: *What do you see down there?*

JAYNE: *Oh, I feel giddy. I just don't want them to touch me.*

KALMAN: *Who's touching you, Jayne?*

JAYNE: *Don't know. Don't want to look.*

KALMAN: *What was the touch like?*

JAYNE: *Hands.*

KALMAN: *Where were you touched?*

JAYNE: *Face.*

KALMAN: *Feel its touch on your face and tell me what you're feeling.*

JAYNE: *[Starts to cry.] Can't feel it because I'm going somewhere. They touched me to start with and now I'm giddy.*

KALMAN: *Where are you?*

JAYNE: *Up.*

KALMAN: *Are you still in the air at Mum's house?*

JAYNE: *High up. Floating.*

KALMAN: *What do you see down there?*

JAYNE: *A box.*

KALMAN: *What is it?*

JAYNE: *If you looked at a garden with a wooden fence from above
    it looks like a box.*

KALMAN: *Whose garden has a fence?*

JAYNE: *Don't know. I feel weird. Forget. You're too close to me, keep
    back!*

KALMAN: *What would happen if I got too close? What would it
    remind you of?*

JAYNE: *Them.*

That is the nearest we came to an admission from Jayne that she saw
something more than the UFOs. After this session the hypnosis was
abandoned for several reasons. Jayne felt we were not going to get any
further, even though she had a conscious desire to know the full story.
She blamed us for that failure because she 'wasn't properly hypnotized'.

In truth, a part of her, the part that determines what our conscious
mind can or cannot cope with, had opened the door a crack but
would not allow it to swing wider open, in case the shock caused
excessive trauma. The 'doorman' knew the full horror that lurked there
in her subconscious.

The stress of remembering had already taken a toll. Jayne's hair had
begun falling out, just like Samantha's in Chapter 2. Once the hypnosis
ceased, it gradually grew back again. Some time later we allowed
Jayne to listen to the tapes we had made of her hypnosis sessions and
she gave us her reaction:

*I was surprised at how quickly I became frightened. Things seemed to
have started before we saw the UFO. I saw Susan by the fire, and then
blackness. I felt there were two Jaynes – one reliving the experience,
and the other in Moyshe's surgery trying to translate and understand it. It felt like my body was reacting to something that my
mind couldn't keep up with. I feel I answered truthfully – I really*

couldn't see what was frightening me.

I felt compelled to say 'mustn't' a lot. It just came out and I don't know why. Maybe I said it because I knew I mustn't give in and make something up. The reason I kept saying that some things must be a dream was because I was very aware that they were not part of the original story. Although under hypnosis I could see them clearly, they did not fit in with what I consciously remember.

I have no idea why I described a white light. It was like a blinding million-watt light wrapped all around me. When I said I was turning, or spinning, the sensation was totally real.

I went ahead with the hypnosis because I wanted to see the UFO clearly again, and believed I could do this without getting frightened. How mistaken I was! I don't really believe everything I said, although I don't feel I made it up either. I'd like to get to the bottom of it, although I doubt I ever will.

The Bonds' UFO experience on that night in 1979 was in some respects just a highlight in a chain of events that had affected the girls and their mother for some years beforehand. It certainly was not the end of it: a great tide of anomalous phenomena was poised to sweep over the family. These events will be described later in the book.

Eventually the girls left home to make lives of their own. Jayne and Laura remained in the area, married and had children. Susan obtained a responsible job with the London Ambulance Service and moved down there to live with her Australian boyfriend. None of that stopped the phenomenon, however. It moved in with them, antagonizing, horrifying and bewildering the girls; even their sceptical partners were not totally immune. Then it started on their children. Yet, despite all this, the girls and their mother retained their objectivity and, more importantly, under the circumstances, their sense of humour.

Fields of Dreams

We all dream at night, but only a fraction of our dreams are remembered. Sometimes we can vividly remember a dream upon waking, but during the process of washing and dressing it evaporates like early morning dew, leaving behind only a tantalizing taste.

Dreams reflect our fears, fantasies and the day's events. They are also a natural mechanism to allow subconscious memories to leach out into the conscious mind, especially when they have been primed to do so between hypnosis sessions. Dreams have such an emotional impact that they naturally demand an explanation or interpretation and often have great significance.

The ancients tried to fathom the future in dreams. They were seen as coded messages from the gods that required priests to interpret their true meaning. The ancient Greeks viewed them as part of the healing process and erected 'sleep temples' where the sick would rest and wait for the gods to speak to them. The Talmud says, 'an uninterpreted dream is like an unopened letter'.

Modern scientific research into dreams has discovered a great deal about when and how often they occur, and what stimuli can affect them, but it has failed to satisfy our desire to know what – if anything – they mean.

Most people today have heard of REM (Rapid Eye Movement) sleep. Researchers have discovered that while we are actually dreaming our eyeballs are active. In NREM (Non-Rapid Eye Movement) or orthodox sleep the mind is engaged in thought, or problem-solving, without the drama of dreaming. The mind is always active and alert, even in sleep.

Early psychoanalysts, led by Sigmund Freud, also tried to find the meaning of dreams with the intention of using them to heal, albeit to cure the diseased mind and not the body, as the Greeks had sought to do. Freud's great work *On The Interpretation of Dreams* concluded that the unconscious, which is highly censored as its contents are often taboo, is at its most accessible during sleep, when barriers come down and suppressed desires, guilt and hidden memories emerge as coded messages.

During our investigation we asked the women of Black Brook Farm to record their dreams for us. Two of Joyce's dreams are described here:

I was in a plane sitting around a table having dinner. We were discussing abductions and if we believed in them. The old lady opposite said she did, and so did her husband. The couple to my right said they both believed it. I felt a bit envious that they were both in agreement. Everyone's belief seemed connected with experience, and particularly air travel. One old lady said, 'It must have happened a lot when I have flown,' and I replied, 'God knows how often it has happened to me, I have flown so much recently.' I had the impression that this particular journey was part of an abduction, and we were waiting for permission to be released.

I went into a room and saw a woman with blonde hair lying on an operating table. Someone standing at her head was pointing a long metal rod, about a foot long with a round flat bit at the end, towards her face. It was to do with anaesthetic, but I knew this was not right. I think this was Moyshe's patellar hammer!

The first dream is interesting. Whitley Strieber also recounts an odd, dream-like memory of an air flight in *Communion*, years before his abduction in 1985. In light of that experience he speculates that the flight was actually a coded memory of an earlier abduction, distorted in order to convince him that nothing strange had occurred. Joyce's other dream seems to be a hybrid of an abduction scenario mixed in with her memory of the hypnosis session she had.

'Up until 25 October 1993 [two weeks before the first hypnosis session] I never had any dreams about UFOs or aliens,' Jayne told us. 'I never dreamed about our encounter. I rarely have bad dreams. These nightmares were out of character.' Her first dream occurred on that date, followed by four more over the next consecutive nights:

1. I was walking across Mum's yard when a helicopter came around the back of the house and landed in the yard. Two men and a woman got out. They were young, pale with dark eyes and long black hair. They wore light-blue padded jackets. The woman said, 'Would you like to see what we really came in?'

I looked across and saw a silver disc-shaped craft. They walked towards it, encouraging me to follow. I didn't want to but I didn't want to be left behind, either. Then we were right up to it, and the woman said, 'You know what comes next, don't you?' I did, but I didn't want them to know. They were trying to get me to admit I knew and wanted me to follow them.

As we stood there they began to change. They became shorter than me, their heads swelled up and their hair disappeared. I woke up very afraid.

2. I dreamed about some horrible ghoul-like creatures which were climbing out of a grave. One looked straight at me. I was frightened by his big grey eyes which lacked whites or pupils.

After this dream, Jayne was woken up with a start by her alarm clock. It had gone off prematurely at 4.25 am. Her husband had already left for work, so Jayne tried to get back to sleep:

Every time I started to fall asleep I got a sensation of something pushing the back of my head hard enough to hurt, followed by the beginnings of a sinking feeling. I managed to stop it by shaking and slapping myself awake. Then I heard something breathing in the corner of the room. I put the light on and the room was very still and quiet. Eventually I fell asleep.

3. I dreamed I was about to be paralysed, so I tried to climb out of bed and fell to the floor unable to move. Something unseen then dragged me along the floor by my dressing-gown neck. I suddenly recovered and ran to phone Laura, but couldn't get through.

Then I saw a bright light coming through the glass kitchen door. I didn't want to look but a voice said I had to. The door opened and a silver craft with legs and a dome landed outside. Then a group of five odd-looking aliens walked in.

They were all different sizes and wore clothes. Some of them had wigs on their bald heads and looked really silly! They sat in the lounge and explained they were dressed like that because they didn't want to alarm me.

The aliens said I was going to help them, and I didn't have any choice. As a goodwill gesture I could go with them and visit anyone I wanted to – but I would be invisible. I said I'd like to see where Kevin, my ex-boyfriend, now is. We went to his parents' house and looked in each of the bedrooms. When I pulled back the covers the people just looked through me – I really was invisible!

By now it was daylight and we found Kevin at a country fair. I went up to him and touched his face. He felt it but couldn't see me. I felt grateful to the aliens, but was still wary of them.

4. A detective was questioning me about why there was a half-hour gap in my diary on 19 November. I was very worried and couldn't explain it. I woke up very concerned and was sick.

5. The big red-and-yellow flashing UFO was outside over the stables. It was just as I remembered it, although I could see it clearer, as I stood in the doorway. There were lots of words coming out of it, long streams of words all around me. I was frightened and woke up, without remembering any of the words.

The following three dreams occurred some time later:

6. I couldn't remember what happened in the dream. Just that there was a big metal room with no furniture, and I was there lying naked on the floor.

7. I dreamed that Sandra Steech and I could fly. We flew to a place where there was an elephant that we were hiding from behind lots of cardboard boxes.

8. I was in a group of four teenagers out hiking when we saw two suspicious men whom we decided to follow. They arrived at a Tardis [the time machine from *Dr Who*] *and inside was a third man who couldn't get out. His face was at a small window. He had horrible large dark eyes and hair. We were too scared to rescue him and ran away, then carried on walking as if nothing had happened.*

In April 1995 – almost a year after the hypnosis sessions had ended – Jayne had another dream based on the UFO encounter at the farm. It some respects it is similar to dream No. 5, except that 'tendrils' replaced the 'streams of words':

We were all standing at the door of Mum's house watching the UFO. It had black tendrils coming out of it. Suddenly Laura's head fell forwards. I saw her neck bend, then mine dropped to the side as it paralysed me. The fear I felt as I stood paralysed, but still aware, was awful. Then the blackness came.

I awoke and the feeling of waiting, whilst paralysed, for it to come and take me, was still very real.

Jayne has also had a number of dreams involving babies. In one she discovered that, without her knowledge, she had given birth to a number of children. This would indicate to some researchers that the dreams are vague memories of having been part of an alien hybrid-breeding programme.

A large number of her dreams hint that Jayne has suffered several UFO entity encounters and abduction experiences. They also convey information about the UFO phenomenon itself. One of the messages seems to be that the aliens are capable of disguising themselves, a theme that crops up often in this book. There are clear supernatural elements, too, such as invisibility and flying.

Jayne's dream of seeing the large UFO again is particularly interesting. She 'remembers' the object pouring information into her mind.

Does this really happen in close encounters? Do the forces behind them put information and ideas directly into the minds of witnesses, perhaps to be activated and remembered at a later date? Before we can even consider such a proposition, we have to know whether these dreams are just fantasies or genuine memories of real events cloaked in dream imagery.

Laura's dreams also indicate that more might have happened that night at Black Brook Farm than the women consciously remembered:

1. For many years I have dreamed of going up vertically. There is a strong sensation of being drawn or sucked upwards. I'm always in the yard at Black Brook. I feel overwhelming panic.

2. I dream I am in Mum's back garden. It's dark and I'm all on my own. I'm so frightened I can't move. I want to reach out for the door handle, which is just within reach, but I can't because I'm paralysed. Had this dream a lot.

3. I often dream of a terrible fear that I can't explain. This fear comes back in my dreams over and over. It's always connected with Black Brook.

4. I dreamed that I was standing by Mum's front gate when something jumped out and grabbed me. It put a plaster right around my hand and I drift into unconsciousness. I found it hard to wake up afterwards, as I felt very groggy.

5. Years ago we went on holiday to the New Forest. We found a wild horse and tried to catch it by putting a rope around its neck. I dream about this field.

In the dream there are several people standing with me looking up at the sky. We're watching two black UFOs. One is always directly above the other but they keep disappearing.

6. I remember this dream vividly even though I had it years ago. I dreamed that I woke up in a glass building. There were hundreds of people lying in rows on the floor. I stood up and looked for a way out. I stepped over them and headed towards an entrance. I went through a large 'kissing-gate' and found myself in an identical room with more people. After I had woken up I felt really groggy, and had to lie down again.

Laura also recalled some images that flashed into her mind when her eyes were closed but she was not yet asleep. In one case she saw a photograph-like image of the side of the UFO that hovered over the farm. Two beings were dropping from it curled up into balls. In another she saw a silver triangular-shaped object. As a door began to open in it, she opened her eyes quickly because she was afraid of what would happen next.

Again, we are left wondering whether these UFO-related images and dreams are nothing more than imagination, or based on real events that have been repressed. Linda Napolitano, an American abductee, described aliens curled up in balls suspended beneath a hovering UFO.

Here is another of Laura's dreams:

On 8 July 1994 I awoke at 3 am, aware of a loud noise directly above the house. The only thing I can compare it to is the noise made by a helicopter. As I sat up in bed the noise gradually faded and everything was silent again. I felt slightly afraid as this occurrence happens quite frequently. Then I fell back to sleep but awoke about an hour later, screaming. I had just had a terrible dream about a fire in my kitchen.

That morning I went out to the local shop with Sonja, one of my daughters. When we arrived back, she ran around to the rear of the house. I heard a terrible explosion and Sonja screaming. Much to my horror, I found the kitchen ablaze. I couldn't do anything for the black smoke and rang the fire brigade. By the time they arrived the kitchen was ruined.

It appears the fire was caused by an electrical fault on the cooker circuit. I suppose we were lucky that neither of us were injured, although Sonja had a narrow escape – the explosion was the window shattering only feet from her.

The literature of the paranormal is filled with similar accounts of premonitions received during sleep. It would seem that the Greeks were right in believing that dreams could predict the future. The dreams of close-encounter and abduction subjects should not be dismissed as mere fantasies.

Chapter 10

Before, During and After

As we have seen, rarely (if ever) are UFO close-encounter experiences single, isolated incidents. When probed, percipients will reveal other anomalous events which have happened in their lives. Joyce, Jayne, Laura and Susan Bond are no exception, but like most other victims, it never occurred to them that there could be a link. Joyce told us: 'I never realized there could be a connection between psychic experiences and UFO sightings.'

During our hypnosis sessions with Jayne she revealed several further incidents. Some had been forgotten entirely, and others first surfaced in dreams between her hypnosis sessions. One particularly interesting memory was set in the Bonds' previous home, in Buckinghamshire:

KALMAN: *Try to take yourself to a place. What about your little bedroom? Tell me what you remember about that room.*

JAYNE: *I saw a tiger in there. They never believed me.*

KALMAN: *Tell me about the tiger.*

JAYNE: *Laura spilled washing-up liquid on my gold carpet. Stained it forever. There was a tiger.*

KALMAN: *Tell me....*

JAYNE: *Over there. Nobody believed me. She said I imagined it, but there were hairs on the floor.*

KALMAN: *Sure there were. What colour was it?*

JAYNE: *Orange. You're going to laugh at me!*

KALMAN: *No one's laughing.*

JAYNE: *Big tiger looking at me.*

KALMAN: *Can you smell it? Tigers often smell. Can you smell the breath of a cat?*

JAYNE: *No.*

KALMAN: *Can you smell his fur?*

JAYNE: *No.*

KALMAN: *What did it feel like, being in the room with a tiger?*

JAYNE: *I edged past it.* [Jayne begins to appear distressed. Kalman soothes her.] *I told Mum the next morning.*

KALMAN: *What did she say?*

JAYNE: *'Don't be stupid.' She said the hairs were from the dog. If I could get past the tiger I'd be all right. It was watching me.*

KALMAN: *What colour are his eyes? Look at those big eyes.*

JAYNE: *Yellowy eyes. Black … eyes.*

KALMAN: *Now what are you reminded of? Say the thought, the fantasy that comes into your mind. They remind you of other eyes, don't they? What are you remembering?* [Jayne starts to cry but Kalman urges her to remember.]

JAYNE: *I don't think I can talk about eyes. I don't like eyes. It can't have been a tiger because tigers don't go into your bedroom. Must have dreamed it.*

KALMAN: *What else do you dream? Take yourself to a place.*

JAYNE: *My bedroom at Mum's house. I don't really want to be in that house.*

KALMAN: *But you're remembering something, aren't you?*

JAYNE: *Lying in bed. I don't like it. It's that thing. Black, but didn't have a face.*

KALMAN: *Think of that standing there.*

JAYNE: *Go, get away! Don't make me think of him ….* [She begins to cry.]

KALMAN: *What are you seeing, Jayne?*

JAYNE: *His black face. Cloaked figure. Face in shadow. Looking at me from the open door. Years later I saw a picture of one. Holding a scythe. 'The death reaper' or something.*

KALMAN: *The Grim Reaper.*

The episode with the tiger is interesting. Whitley Strieber described seeing an owl on his windowsill the night of his abduction. Strieber, along with American researchers like Budd Hopkins, believes that these are 'screen memories'. In order to disguise the true nature of the experience, the victim remembers seeing an animal instead of an alien being.

Jayne's childhood experience of 'the Grim Reaper' may be connected to her reaction to a photograph she saw in a book many years later. In 1993 Peter Hough and Jenny Randles produced *The Afterlife*, and Peter presented Jayne with a copy of the book. He learned afterwards what happened when she browsed through it.

On page 109 of the book is a photograph taken in the church at Newby, in Yorkshire. It shows an extremely tall hooded figure swathed in a black robe or cloak. The face is covered in a white mask, similar to those worn by members of the Ku Klux Klan, with two black holes for the eyes.

Jayne had hysterics when she turned to this photograph and saw the mask. She later covered the offending picture with a drawing of the comical television character 'Mr Blobby'. Interestingly, she had first seen the picture before the hypnosis sessions began, and it had no effect on her. The reaction came when she saw it afterwards.

Why this extreme reaction to a picture? What exactly did it represent in Jayne's mind? Obviously something extremely unpleasant. The figure is like her Grim Reaper in many ways, but the black holes in the mask are more reminiscent of the large black eyes of UFO entities.

Under hypnosis, Jayne described to us another encounter she had at her home in Buckinghamshire. At the time she was playing in her back garden, next to some woodland. As she ran through the shrubs, Jayne suddenly stopped dead. Five metres (5 yd) away was the figure of a 'man' wearing a short white coat. She told Kalman that he 'didn't have any legs'. Jayne added that he was about thirty-five, stocky, with short brown hair and that he was 'floating'.

It might seem that Jayne had a monopoly on anomalous experiences, so they might reasonably be explained as hallucinations. However, this bias arose simply because we were able to do a great deal of work with Jayne, while her mother and sisters were less willing to co-operate. Indeed, one of the reasons why Jayne's sister Laura did not become personally involved with our work was because she was even more affected by the experiences than Jayne. It came as no surprise to discover that the family had experienced further strange incidents. The number and extent of these events, however, was quite staggering. Unfortunately, none of the percipients have so far been able to produce any concrete evidence, although there is no reason to doubt the sincerity of all concerned. Joyce told us: 'I always thought our house was haunted, but I never connected it with the UFO. I'm not exactly sure when it started, but it was about the same time.'

The first of these experiences involved a mysterious glowing white object which was sighted twice in 1982, according to Jayne:

Laura, Susan and I were in bed upstairs when we were awoken by a 'howl' and, I think, footsteps. We looked out the window across the garden and saw something about 50 yards away. It resembled a white glowing pillar about five and a half feet high. We leaned out of the window but couldn't make it out. To reassure ourselves, we decided it must be a white horse standing in the field, but when we went outside to check we found the gate shut and all the horses locked away.

The second time the apparition appeared there were three witnesses unconnected with the family. Two 14-year-old girls and one of the girls' 16-year-old boyfriend were seeing to a pony in its stable near the garden. Suddenly they saw a glowing white shape float down the old railway embankment, over the fence and across the garden towards them. They ran home and told Susan Bond at school the following day. These witnesses knew nothing about the previous sighting.

It was not until August 1990 that the apparition was spotted again. By this time the Bond girls had grown up and left the farm.

Laura had had a row with her husband and was staying at the farm while her parents were away on holiday. According to Jayne, who learned of the episode from Laura, her sister let the dog out at 11.30 pm and 15 minutes later opened the door to let him in. The animal rushed back into the house with his hackles up. Laura thought he was still worked up because of a fight he had had with her own dog some six hours earlier.

For reasons she cannot explain, Laura then switched off every light in the house and walked to the stairs in the dark. As she prepared to climb them, she saw a white glowing thing pressed up against the frosted glass of the back door. It was about 2 metres (6 feet) high and 60 cm (2 feet) thick, and solid-looking. Laura went upstairs, dragging the dog with her, still without switching on any lights, and had a restless night filled with bad dreams. She dreamed that an alien hit her on the head with an implement, driving her into blackness. For several nights afterwards she would feel something like a blow to the head when she went into her bedroom.

By morning Laura had completely forgotten about the incident. In the afternoon something triggered off the memory and she checked the gate, which was still closed. The dog was reluctant to go into the garden, preferring to stay close to the back door. Laura's husband William came around later, with her sister Jayne, who said:

Laura wasn't frightened at the time, but when we questioned her, she was. She swore it was the truth. . . . That night we decided to explore the garden to see if we could find anything. William and Laura went out first. Just as I was on the threshold all the lights in the house went out. We screamed, then plucked up the courage to go back inside. William examined the fuse-box, but it was OK. About an hour later the lights came back on again. Half of the village had been plunged into darkness when an electricity substation on the far side of the railway embankment had mysteriously caught fire.

Frightened, but still trying to discover the truth, they later tried an experiment with a sheet and a torch but could not re-create the glowing object.

In 1993 Jayne, her sceptical husband Andrew and daughter Jasmine were witness to the phenomenon. They were looking after the farm while Jayne's parents were away. Jayne and Andrew were in the lounge with the curtains open watching television. Suddenly, they jumped up, startled, when something white rushed past one of the windows. Andrew exclaimed, 'What the hell was that?' Jayne went out into the yard but there was no sign of it.

'I got the best look,' she said, 'but, most importantly, Andrew and Jas saw it too. We worked out it was about my height, creamy white, solid, and moving at running speed. The gate was still shut.'

Jayne told us that Black Brook Farm was also haunted by a poltergeist:

It started off around 1979 quite harmlessly, but by 1984 it had us terrified. At the time we were trying to find a medium who would get rid of the spook but Laura was scared this would make it madder, and we didn't know where we would be sending it.

Joyce Bond described some typical poltergeist activity at Black Brook:

Most of the things seemed to happen upstairs in the old part of the building. My husband and I sleep in the new extension on the ground floor. The children were often frightened, so I would sometimes sleep upstairs. I once heard a small sound of laughter, sniffing, had an earring pulled, and felt something on the end of the bed. Often I awoke in the night with a start, my heart racing. One constant apparition has been the spook cat.

We have all seen it, even the dog. It always appears from the autumn onwards – just something black, darting, usually in the kitchen. I must add we have six black-and-white cats, but these live outside, coming in once a day to feed, then straight out again. At the beginning of February 1991 my three-year-old granddaughter Jasmine was adamant she saw a cat while playing in the larder.

There is an intriguing story told to me by a local farmer whose uncle once lived here. The story goes that a witch named Margaret Clough, a previous tenant of Black Brook, could turn herself into a black cat. When the cat appeared at milking time the cows would not give milk. On one occasion a pitchfork was thrown at the cat. It was later noticed that Margaret Clough had the marks of the pitchfork on her hands. The farmer who told me the story had no idea we had seen a cat. I wanted to ask more, but tragically he was killed only a week later while driving the school bus.

In August 1992 Susan came up from London to spend some time at Black Brook Farm. The first night she woke up, terrified by something unknown. The following night she slept downstairs in the dining-room. She woke up to see Jason the dog levitating up and down on the end of the bed. After that the dog became increasingly nervous.

The most recent event occurred in early 1996. Mr and Mrs Bond sleep in the downstairs extension at the rear of the farm. Joyce was alarmed one night to hear a noise like someone charging at the back door. As the door is mainly glass she was surprised, on inspection, to find it intact. There was no evidence of a prowler. A few nights later the same charging noise was heard, at her bedroom window this time. Again, there was no damage.

At the rear of the house is a large shed used for storage. The roof had been leaking for some time, but rather than renew the roofing felt, Mr Bond decided to nail corrugated iron on top of it. Several nights after the window incident, the Bonds heard a noise which they took for thunder. It was not repeated and they went to sleep. The following morning they were shocked to find that the corrugated-iron roof had been lifted up through 90 degrees so that it leaned against the roof of the adjoining building (see plate section).

Was the wind responsible for these three incidents? The Bonds have said that none of the nights in question were windy or stormy. The shed roof weighs about a tonne and the building is protected at the rear and on one side by trees. If it was the wind, why did it not disturb a pile of straw nearby, or dislodge a halter hanging precariously on a nail just centimetres away from the roof?

On other occasions, the girls and their mother have experienced an incubus-like entity on or in bed with them. According to centuries-old tradition, an incubus is a male demon lover of women. Its female counterpart is the succubus, which preys on men and is often referred to as 'the Old Hag'. Peter Hough has a growing file of cases involving such entities, although in the majority, including that of the Bonds, there is no sexual dimension. The encounters can be quite alarming, nevertheless.

In 1984, when she was 15, Susan had this experience:

I had gone to bed and fallen asleep when I awoke with a start to find I was being strangled. I remember being in pitch darkness, pinned down, with additional pressure on my neck, unable to move. I don't remember struggling or how long the sensation lasted. But I did remember the feeling of relief and peace afterwards. I then went back to sleep. I didn't say anything until much later, when my sister mentioned it had happened to her. It puzzles me that I don't remember very much and that it becomes increasingly vague as I try to recall details.

This is what Jayne told us:

Both Mum and I have felt something in bed with us. Most of us have felt something sitting on our feet when there was nothing visible. Mum's bed has vibrated and all of us have felt our earrings being tugged at night.

How it began is hard to remember. I think I would be asleep and gradually wake up, bit by bit realizing I was pinned to the bed. It felt like two fingers squeezing the top of my shoulders near my neck on either side. Although I felt completely physically restrained, I only felt pressure at this point, where it hurt. I tried to wriggle free but my arms were stuck to my sides. I wouldn't say I was paralysed, just totally restrained. My mouth and eyes were covered so I saw only blackness. I could hear my own muffled cries for help. It would go on for a couple of minutes.

No one ever came to my aid. On one occasion I just gave up and waited for it to finish. Then suddenly it would just stop and apart from a pounding heart I would be OK. I was very frightened while it lasted. Then I would just doze off.

One night in May 1992, I woke to feel something touching me through the duvet. It felt like someone playing the piano on my left side. I felt quite brave so I thought I would grab 'it'. When I went to move my arm I realized I was almost totally paralysed. Everything except my eyes – all I could see was the pillow. When I tried to scream even my voice wouldn't work. I had to lie there while it ran its 'fingers' up and down me. After two minutes it stopped.

In 1992, Joyce told us, 'Only recently I had the horrible feeling of something moving about on my bed.' Some time in 1995 Jayne saw a hairy arm disappearing under the bed after feeling it touch her.

All three girls have experienced a 'sinking feeling', sometimes coupled with paralysis. This often occurs at the onset of an experience. Jayne told us how it felt:

I have had the 'sinking feeling' twice this year [1992]. It was a very violent, sucking-down feeling. I fought back up again and was pulled down a couple of times more. It's absolutely terrifying. It frightens me more than anything.

In December 1992 she told us:

A couple of weeks ago something horrible happened. I woke up after Andrew had gone to work and leaned over his side to look at the clock. As I did so something touched me on the forehead like a cold pen. I lay back and thought, What the hell was that? and then I was overwhelmed by the sinking feeling. I didn't have the strength to get up, I just had to put up with it.

One afternoon in July 1993 Jayne was feeling under the weather and went to lie down on her old bed. She was positioned on her left side, facing away from the door, and had been there a few minutes when she realized someone was sitting on the end of the bed. She could just see white curly hair, like a woman's perm.

I went to sit up and – surprise, surprise – I was paralysed. Then a voice said, 'You know who I am, don't you?' It sounded female, and I replied, 'Yes, I know who you are.' Then it said, 'You've got to believe in me.' I said I wouldn't and it paralysed me deeper. Then I thought that if I told it I believed in Jesus it might leave me alone. I said the Lord's Prayer and repeated bits of hymns I remembered from school. This made it angry and it got a firmer grip on me.

Jayne tried desperately to free herself. Then she had an idea. Perhaps she could escape if she turned her thoughts away from it. She visualized an empty blackboard and the paralysis stopped, but when she moved 'it' gripped her again. Jayne repeated this procedure several times until finally she was free. She sat up in bed for a few moments, then lay down again – and found she could not move.

'It persisted in saying that I had to believe in it, and I kept saying I believed in God,' she told us.

Then Jayne decided she would try to leave her body. She lifted up her hand. Her physical arm remained on the pillow. Jayne showed her annoyance by calling the entity 'ugly'. She could not see its face because of the folds in the quilt, but she had an overwhelming feeling that it was grotesque and incredibly old. Jayne tried the blackboard trick again and, the moment she was free, leaped up. 'It' had gone again – this time for good.

The entire experience had lasted about 45 minutes. When she told Andrew about it, he claimed that during that time he had walked into the room to check if Jayne was all right and had found her asleep. Jayne suggested that as she was lying on her side, facing away from the door, he might have mistakenly thought she was sleeping peacefully when in fact she was in the grip of paralysis.

The next day the side of Jayne's face that had been on the pillow swelled up and turned red. It began to itch and remained in this state for several days.

The episode is reminiscent of the scene in *Peter Pan* where Tinkerbell, the fairy, begins to fade away. She can be saved only if the children in the audience believe she is real. Jayne and Laura have often said that when they stop believing in the phenomenon, 'nothing happens.' It may be that a sinister symbiotic relationship exists between ourselves and supernatural or paranormal entities: without our belief they cannot exist in our reality, although it is hard to see what benefit such a relationship might have for us.

Laura described one of her 'attacks', which happened on Sunday, 5 September 1993. She and her husband were watching television in their lounge when she experienced a twisting sensation:

I've had it quite often and I don't really mind it. I feel as though I am all twisted up and have to look at myself to see how I'm sitting. I felt sort of suspended to my left with legs crossed (although they weren't) and wiggled my fingers to check they were still there. I told my husband and we joked together. He thinks I'm very strange.

It lasted ten minutes. At 9 pm they decided to go to bed and watch a film, but by 9.30 pm they were both asleep. Two hours later Laura was disturbed by an intense itch in her right ear.

Suddenly I was plunged into the sinking paralysis feeling. My only thought was to get myself out of it. I was hurting. I wanted to alert my husband and tried to grunt, but I couldn't move a muscle. Three times I fought it off, but each time I was progressively weaker. Then I heard a female voice, inside of me. It said: 'This time don't fight it, let go, it won't hurt.' So I did.

At that moment I felt I had left my body. Then I was spinning round and round. I was thinking, this is what dying is like. I realized I had let it get the better of me and I felt cheated. There were hundreds of blue flashing lights all around me and I was spinning inside of them. They were so bright that white bits shot out of them. Then blankness.

Some time passed. I feel that maybe I blacked out, died or just fell asleep. Suddenly I was back in bed. I had to fight off the paralysis, then my eyes opened. The time was 12.23 am.

The least affected by any of the phenomena seems to be Susan, but in January 1994 she experienced both paralysis and the sinking sensation in her house in London:

I woke up sideways across the bed and for a short while couldn't move, even though I was wide awake. Why was I in this position? That weekend I went up to Black Brook Farm and had a terrible 'dream'. I had been asleep when suddenly I felt this awful pulling feeling on my body. I was in bed yet I felt I was being violently spun round and round while at the same time I was being dragged downwards. It was very frightening.

One of the features of this complex case is the way the strange experiences have spread out from Black Brook Farm, apparently following the girls and affecting their friends, children and even their sceptical husbands. It almost seems as though the women are infected in some way and anyone with whom they have an emotional bond is also affected. In May 1992 Jayne told us that her sister Susan had seen an 'alien' while camping with her boyfriend. 'It was hovering over her, looking at her curiously', she said. 'She yelled at Alex to get it away from her, but he couldn't see it.'

Jayne also reports that Susan's friend Jo has experienced the sinking feeling and that Jo's boyfriend Martin saw an 'alien' at the end of his bed in Australia. They are apparently sincere and very frightened.

One night in 1996 Susan woke up in her London home and saw a white glowing thing hovering above the bed. With some difficulty, she woke her boyfriend and told him what she had seen, but he explained it away, saying she had seen their pet cat. The experience went right out of Susan's mind until several days later, when she was standing in the bedroom doorway. A terrible feeling of horror took hold of her as the incident came flooding back.

On 17 February 1991 Jayne had a strange experience on waking up in the house she shares with her husband:

I know it sounds crazy, but I woke and saw a big tube full of blue stars coming through the ceiling to the bedroom floor. I desperately tried to wake Andrew by hitting and thumping him, but it had no effect. I curled up under the sheets and when I peeped out it was right at the end of the bed. I didn't dare look again.

How many times have subjects tried desperately to waken their partners, to no avail? Jayne thinks she may have imagined the 'tube', confusing it with a blue bulb she has in her night-light.

On the same night, however, Jayne had a poltergeist experience involving her 11-month-old son Christopher:

During the night Christopher woke up screaming. I have never heard him cry like that before. I went into his room and he leaped at me and clung. I took him to my bed and eventually he slept, clutching my hand to his chest. He has never behaved like this before. My husband, who is always very sceptical, agrees that he was terrified.

Andrew went to work at 3.20 am, and at 5.50 am I put Christopher back in his own room. By now I was wide awake. Back in bed I heard a sound like bits of paper being folded behind me. Every time I looked, it stopped, like someone playing a game. Then something invisible swirled into the room, went across the end of the bed, turned and stopped. Afterwards I checked the windows were closed.

In her letter of 10 May 1992, Jayne reported a recent incident where a shelf 'flew' off the kitchen wall while the family were having lunch. 'It broke my favourite china. Andrew agrees it flew horizontally away from the wall and then down.'

Three months later Jayne had a further experience to report. 'It was probably some sort of waking dream but it scared me into a panic,' she rationalized.

I awoke during the night and decided to turn over and face Andrew. I shut my eyes, turned over, then when I opened them to look at him, I got the shock of my life – it wasn't Andrew!

It was some man of about 50. He turned his head towards me and smiled – leered, really – and I said, 'Oh, my God!' I never got out of bed so quickly in all my life. I headed for the door, shouting, when Andrew said, 'It's all right now, it's all right, he's gone.' I was so relieved. My heart took ages to stop thumping. It must have been a dream, but the way he looked at me still gives me the creeps.

In December 1992 Jayne notified us of two recent experiences:

On Tuesday night something horrible happened. I awoke with a start, very frightened. The night-light wasn't on, so there wasn't much illumination. There was something big and dark standing next to my side of the bed. I flung myself over to Andrew. It was a man, I think, leaning over him, glowing slightly and transparent. This wasn't a dream; I was wide awake and absolutely terrified.

I shook Andrew and shouted that there was a 'man'. Eventually he mumbled, 'It's all right, he's gone now.' But it hadn't, it was still there! I was shouting and sobbing, my heart was pounding. Eventually the man faded away. Andrew doesn't remember anything about that night.

In October 1994 Jayne told us that she had been having 'sort of night terrors'. Andrew had woken during the night to find his wife throwing off the quilt, and screaming, 'Get them off me!' It took him a long time to calm her down. She has no memory of this at all. She also gave details of a new type of experience:

I woke up in a totally different room. It was all oak beams and big wooden furniture. I got up and walked around. The window was in a different place to mine, and there was some sacking hanging on it. I was so scared I just looked straight ahead and headed for where my door would be. It was only when I walked into the hall-way that everything reverted to normal.

Jayne says she was wide awake, but wonders if her perceptions were still keyed into a dream she might have been having.

Budd Hopkins (see plate section) was the first American researcher to highlight the cases of child abductees. He found that the children of abductees became abductees themselves. Hopkins and others, including David Jacobs and John Mack, believe that alien beings target families and over several generations regularly take members away for experimental purposes. Of course this raises the question of how well-insulated the children are from their parents' beliefs. In the late 1990s the media regularly bombard audiences with UFO and abduction imagery.

Joyce Bond and her daughters assured us that they have been careful to ensure their children are not aware of their experiences. They have become enmeshed in them, nevertheless. Jayne told us what happened to her daughter, Jasmine in the summer of 1991, when she was about three and a half:

One night Jasmine woke up screaming and shouting, 'I can't see! I can't see!' It was probably a nightmare. Then, one morning, she said, 'I saw them last night.' 'Who?' I asked. 'The dollies.'

Jasmine always called dolls 'babies' and still does. Then she started talking about 'Katy'. She said Katy wore a white dress and had long brown hair. We all got quite sick of Katy! I went to playschool, but the Katy there wasn't a friend, nor did she fit the description. I thought that Katy was probably an imaginary friend.

Jayne, Susan and their mother, Joyce, went to hear Budd Hopkins lecture in Sheffield about childhood abductions. Back home, they carried out a test on Jasmine which Hopkins had described. It involved showing the child a series of pictures, one which showed the common large-headed Grey entity. The women asked Jasmine to comment on the pictures. When the child came to the picture of the Grey, she referred to it as a 'witchie' and claimed it had come into her bedroom. The conversation between mother and daughter reportedly went like this:

'What colour was the "witchie"?'
'Blue.'
'What were the eyes like?'
'Big, black.'

'What was the nose like?'
'He have no nose, have two holes.'
'What was the hair like?'
'Have no hair.'
'What were the hands like?'
'They have no thumbs.'
'What does witchie do in your room?'
'Rubs mud on my back.'
'Does it hurt?'
'No. He says, "You can tell your mummy in the morning."'
'When do you see Katy?'
'Comes with the witchie in my room.'
'What does Katy look like?'
*'Same as me, with white dress and long brown hair and funny
   eyes.'*

Jayne commented that her daughter explained that there are two Katys, one at playschool and the one who comes to her room. Jasmine would not elaborate about the witchie's eyes except to say they were 'big'. Jayne's letter continued:

Jasmine says Katy always comes with the witchie and they play. The witchie always rubs mud on her back. She says Katy goes out through the window, and Jasmine through the door. Then Katy and witchie fly away in a grey-and-white 'plane'. Later she talked about 'Tarim', who didn't play with her and who looked like witchie.

After a while happily discussing it, she told me she didn't want to talk any more – and she hasn't, not a word. No more Katy. I don't think she remembers now. I believe Jasmine did experience something, but I don't want it to happen to her. I'm pleased it's stopped.

Katy had not gone away for good, however. It seems she had just moved house. Jayne explained:

Just after 'Katy' had left my house, Laura's daughter Sonja, then aged one and a half, started calling Katy's name at night, and shouting, 'Hope [Help], Mummy, Mummy, hope!'

Laura herself has had a terrible time. It started with strange orange flashing lights on the back door which went before she could open it. Strange noises on the roof, then footsteps, hearing Sonja laugh and saying 'Hello'. Laura thinks that if you talk about it, it happens. Nothing has happened since baby Emily was born, but she is really scared.

Laura told us about these experiences:

I awoke one night to hear the sound of tiny footsteps in the bathroom. Having a sudden urge to go to the toilet, I made my way towards the noise. I stopped outside Sonja's bedroom as I could hear her talking. She was only a year old but was saying, 'Hello, I'm Sonja.' I then noticed a blue light coming from under the door, but even so my reaction was to visit the bathroom and then go back to bed.

The next morning I felt ashamed for not entering her room, but the fear of what I might see was too overwhelming. I will never forgive myself. Since then she has woken up on several occasions full of fear, shouting 'Help!'.

Shortly after that episode I had a very strange 'dream'. I can't say I was fully asleep, nor can I say I was awake, or I'm sure I would have reacted differently.

Something came up the stairs, sat on the edge of the bed and took my hand. I thought it was an alien. Its fingers were long and cold, and wrapped right around mine. We floated downstairs and into the kitchen. Then it wanted me to go out into the garden, and for the first time I felt afraid.

I struggled and broke free, and I felt its annoyance. Then I was back in my bed, trying to convince myself it was just a weird dream, but I knew it would be back.

About a week later it did come back, entering my room while I was 'asleep' and taking my hand. When I came too I knew it was there but couldn't open my eyes. It was talking to me and I don't think I was supposed to wake up while it was still there. Because I did, I could remember a little of what it had said.

It said it was going to visit all of us, and mentioned our eyes and stomachs. I started to panic and again felt its anger. As it left I felt a cold rush of air and opened my eyes to see the door move.

The episode where Laura held the hand of the alien and floated down the stairs has echoes in other cases we have investigated. Stephen Pal, for instance, believes he and his family were abducted when he was four years old. Twenty-two years later he was married with a young son. On 24 December 1990 he awoke from a light sleep to see a Grey in the bedroom. The next thing he remembers is standing at the side of the bed with his wife, arguing that they had to go with the being:

I took Anne by the hand, and in turn my other hand was taken by the alien. The being led us onto the landing, then we glided downstairs over to the kitchen door. I was surprised that we did not stop to unlock it, but just passed through it as if it was not there.

Some years before her abduction in 1976, Shelley, who was introduced earlier in the book, woke up in the night with the strange conviction that she could float downstairs. She woke her sister and, taking her hand, stepped off the top stair and glided to the bottom. When they stepped into the lounge and told their parents what they had just done, the girls were told to get back into bed. Shelley's sister backed up the story when she was interviewed by Peter Hough.

A near-identical story was told to us by Abigail, whom we also discussed earlier. She claims that one night when she was a child, she woke up and felt compelled to go out onto the landing. There she met her brother, who had experienced the same compulsion. They took hands and floated downstairs. When Abigail confronted her brother the following morning, he denied it had happened, but said he had dreamed it. That they should both have had the same dream on the same night is almost as unbelievable as Abigail's assertion that they actually floated.

In April 1994 Laura related another incident that happened at her home. Sonja woke her up at 5.15 am complaining that she had wet her bed, something she rarely did. The child climbed into bed and wrapped her arms around Laura:

Then I heard whispering. At first I thought it was Sonja, but then I realized it was a continuous line of words. There were no sentences. I wanted to turn over, and realized I couldn't. A tingling that started in my hands spread until I became paralysed.

At this point, Laura 'remembered' seeing a photograph, 'a large Polaroid' of Sonja standing next to a very tall man:

I thought how tiny she looked compared to him. I felt that he was friendly and wasn't going to hurt her. He looked like the apparition on the tube train in the film Ghost.

Laura concentrated on the whispering and managed to make out some of the words. It was Sonja, and she was saying, over and over, 'I can see a motor bike mummy.' Laura listened, but could not hear a motor-cycle. Then she started getting what she calls 'the RVDF' – rapid violent downward force:

I had to start fighting. Sonja's hand was still on me but it seemed really hot and heavy, not like Sonja's at all. Then the RVDF intensified and I realized I wasn't going to get out of it. As I was going I felt I was in the yard at Mum's house, driving into the earth.

At some point I dreamed I was in the yard looking down into a slatted window. It was very bright inside and there was a lot of activity. A voice said, 'You shouldn't be looking through there.'

Laura woke up at 8 am, groggy, with a stiff neck. She did not think of her dream until an hour and a half later, when they reached Black Brook Farm:

When I suddenly remembered it I got an instant headache. Sonja also complained of a headache. I suggested that maybe she hadn't slept well. She replied: 'After I snuggled up in bed with you, I had a bad dream. I dreamt some witches came and tried to eat me.' She also said that there was a dragon too, and she thought she was watching a video.

At that time Laura did not take much interest in other people's close-encounter or abduction experiences, mainly out of fear. She had not read any books or watched anything on television connected with the subject. She told us that her husband was 'completely switched off to it' and added, 'In fact, I don't tell him any-thing now, and he doesn't know that Sonja is starting to be affected.'

When Joyce's mother came up to see the family shortly after their trip to the UFO conference, she asked Jayne what aliens are sup-posed to look like. Jasmine was in earshot at the time. Jayne told us:

Before I could reply, Jasmine ran up behind me and put her hands over my mouth. I changed the subject and she wandered off. There was no point in discussing it with Nan, as she would never ever believe or understand. I think Jasmine realized this.

The next day Jasmine said she had been frightened at night. She said she had heard an apple drop off the tree in the garden. When she looked out she saw the moon in the garden. I asked very casu-ally what exactly she had seen. She said the moon was yellow and looked like a balloon, then it flew away.

Things went quiet for a while with Sonja, but after the kitchen fire, the child started talking about visitors again:

She talks about someone called 'Allan'. It appears Allan is a little girl who comes to her room at night. Allan can 'jump up into the sky'. She also says she has been in a plane and seen the clouds. Allan looks like her but isn't.

Jayne and Laura seem to share experiences even though they live some distance apart. On many occasions when Jayne has been paralysed, Laura will report to her sister the following day how, the previous night, she had woken up unable to move.

In January 1996 Jayne woke in the night and saw what looked like a mass of glowing, wriggling worms on a chest of drawers in her bedroom. She climbed out of bed and went over to the chest. When she reached out and touched them, they disappeared. Jayne said she was perfectly awake during the experience. The following day, quite spontaneously, Laura told her sister of a strange dream she had had that night. She had dreamed of a mass of glowing wrig-gling worms.

In 1995 a much more bizarre event visited both households. After watching a late-night film, Jayne and Andrew went immediately to bed. Just as they lay down to sleep there was 'an enormous clatter in the hall, like cardboard boxes falling'. They jumped up and looked for the source of the noise, but found nothing. A further mystery added to the confusion. The film had ended at 11.30 pm. Ten minutes at most had elapsed, but the clock said 12.30 am. They checked all the clocks in the house and their watches and they all confirmed the time. Jayne and her husband could not understand it, as she told us:

We were both wide awake and definitely did not fall asleep. Indeed, we had gone to bed that minute. In the morning I checked the loft in case something had toppled over to account for the noise, but there was nothing that could have fallen.

The couple live in a detached bungalow, so it could not have been their neighbours they heard. Later that day, Jayne, having completely forgotten the noise in the hall and the time loss, was telling her mother about the film. Then Laura arrived and commented that it was unusual for her sister to stay up so late to watch television. Jayne countered by saying, 'Not really, half-past eleven isn't that late.' It was Laura's turn to be indignant. She was certain the film had finished at 1.30 am. Jayne explained:

After some rowing we checked the previous day's paper and found that it had finished at 11.30 pm. Laura said that at the end of the film she switched off the television and went to let the dog out. She remembers seeing 'stars' shining on the back door. When she looked at her watch it said 1.30 am and she went to bed. It's obvious it doesn't take two hours to walk ten yards!

It was while Laura was telling her story that Jayne remembered what had happened in her house. Alan remembered the incident too, but acted totally uninterested, even though he could not explain it.

Many of these episodes seem indicative of partially remembered abduction episodes. Is the family a victim of intergenerational intrusions by beings from 'elsewhere'? Has a rift opened up allowing unknown forces to enter the area of Black Brook Farm?

11

The Phenomenal Intimidators

There is another aspect of UFO abductions and encounters which we believe further illustrates their paranormal origin. UFO literature is full of accounts of witness intimidation by strange-looking 'officials'. These stories first came to the attention of American ufologists in the 1960s. Some witnesses described how men in smart business suits visited them even before they had spoken to anyone about their experience.

These 'men' wear black suits, shoes and ties and white shirts. Their shoes are shiny and, like their clothing, appear brand new. The men arrive in black cars that look in showroom condition even though they are old models. Their behaviour is bizarre. Because of their funereal dress and intimidating air, they have been dubbed 'the Men in Black', or MIB. No case illustrates the bizarreness of these American encounters more than the one involving Dr Herbert Hopkins.

In 1976 Dr Hopkins was helping investigators in Maine, USA, by conducting hypnotic-regression experiments. One evening when his family had gone out to see a film, he received a telephone call. The caller said he was a New Jersey ufologist with an interest in Hopkins' current case and asked if he could come over and discuss it. Hopkins agreed and the caller said he would come around right away. He arrived sooner than Dr Hopkins expected.

As he turned from the telephone to switch on the outside light, a man was already climbing the steps to the door. This was long before mobile public telephones were available. It was impossible for the man to have reached the house from the nearest telephone in such a short time.

Standing facing Dr Hopkins was a man wearing a black suit, hat, tie and shoes and a white shirt. The clothes looked brand new and he reminded Hopkins of an undertaker. Like most people who meet the MIB, the doctor behaved in a strangely subdued fashion.

Even when the visitor took off his hat to reveal that he was completely bald, and accidentally smeared his lipstick, Dr Hopkins did not react, but carried on discussing the case as if everything was completely normal. After a time the man's speech became slurred. He complained of a loss of energy, then left. Afterwards, the doctor was so affected by the experience that he destroyed the audiotapes of the hypnosis sessions.

The same year that Dr Herbert Hopkins had his experience, the 17-year-old receptionist called Shelley referred to in previous chapters suffered at the hands of the MIB after a UFO experience. In her case there were two witnesses: her mother and father.

Shelley told Peter Hough that she was walking home from work on 23 January 1976 after alighting from a bus when she saw a light hovering over the nearby Rumworth Lodge Reservoir. Suddenly the light flew towards her and resolved into a classic 'flying saucer' with portholes and tripod legs. She arrived at her parents' house much later than expected; her mother had called the police, thinking she had been attacked.

Two weeks after Shelley's sighting there was a knock at the door. Shelley's father opened it to two men wearing black trenchcoats. They said they wanted to talk to the girl about her sighting. When her father refused, one of them said they would return later and *make sure* she spoke to them. At this point, Shelley, who had been listening on the stairs, asked her father to let them in.

During the ensuing four and a half hours one of the men did all the talking while the other sat on a chair with a black box on his knee, staring at the girl. He said the box was a tape recorder, but during the entire evening no tape was replaced or even turned over. The man who did the talking had only one arm. He claimed he was a Commander in the RAF and had lost the arm in action. 'Commander' is a naval term.

After admiring a bust of Sir Winston Churchill in the room, the Commander questioned Shelley about the sighting and tried to convince her she had wrongly identified a weather balloon. When she denied this he told her she was a liar and had made up the whole story. Shelley burst into tears and he then agreed she had seen something, but it was actually a secret experimental aircraft. He warned her not to speak to anyone else about it.

What were Shelley's parents doing while their teenage daughter was being interrogated? Most of the time they sat on the settee, watching in silence. When her father asked the MIB exactly who they were, the Commander said, 'We just investigate these things.' He provided no identification when asked to do so.

Shelley's father was acting completely out of character. A business man with a staff of 15 salesmen, he had a reputation for not suffering fools gladly. Yet he allowed two strangers to bully his daughter while he sat by and watched.

Shelley remembers some odd things about the visitors. 'Even though it was raining their coats were dry when they stepped inside,' she remarked. 'A third man drove them away in an old-fashioned black car, which looked like it was new.'

Under hypnosis she revealed that the Commander was talking to her 'twice' – verbally and through direct communication with her mind. She could not recall what the subliminal message was.

Philip Spencer, who apparently took a photograph of one of his abductors on Ilkley Moor, was also visited by two such 'officials'. One Friday night in January 1988, six weeks after his UFO experience, Philip answered the door to two middle-aged men smartly dressed in business suits. They showed him identity cards bearing the letters 'MoD' across the top. Beneath photographs of the men were the names 'Jefferson' and 'Davies'.

He invited them inside when Jefferson (who did most of the talking) said they had come to interview him about his experience. Philip never thought to ask how they had found out, even though he believed at the time that only four investigators knew his identity.

The men wanted to know about his UFO sighting and asked if any photographs had been taken. He admitted that one had been taken and Jefferson asked to examine it. When Philip explained it was with 'a friend' – in fact, Hough had taken it to be analysed – the men lost interest and left.

Philip found the men's behaviour during the interview somewhat odd. They seemed fascinated by ordinary domestic appliances. For instance, seemed fascinated with Philip's electric fire, and asked him how it worked. Crucially, although she took no part in the interview, Mrs Spencer verified that two men had indeed called that night.

Armed with a date, a description and the men's names, Hough wrote to the Ministry of Defence asking them to verify the visit. They claimed that no one from the department had called on Mr Spencer. In reply to a second letter they said that the layout of the identity cards did not conform to current or past designs. However, they continued to ignore repeated requests to comment on the names.

While Janet (see Chapter 3) was a college student, on several occasions a car driven by a man dressed in black followed her. In the autumn of 1992 she and her boyfriend Harry had a strange experience while parked in a country lane near Manchester Airport. Harry described the incident under hypnosis:

It's our favourite 'cuddle spot'. The sun's over the horizon and it's nearly dark. We've got the windows closed and we're just talking. There's a car without any lights coming slowly towards us. It reminds me of a Chicago gangster's car. I get the impression there are two people inside. Why is it moving so slowly? Why doesn't he drive past and leave us alone?

Janet added in an interview: 'It was too dark down the lane to have seen without lights. The car went in the direction of the airport. We drove after it but could find no trace.'

Laura Bond had a run-in with the MIB in 1993, although she had never heard of the term, and tried to find a rational explanation for what she saw.

This is what happened while Laura was out walking her dog, in broad daylight, along a road on the outskirts of the village:

The main road was quiet at the time when a car approached me. It was driving very slowly. I immediately felt nervous when I noticed two men in the front dressed identically in black suits with dazzling white shirts. To my horror the car stopped beside me.

It was very long, with three black side windows, and a 'V' stuck on the back. I later discovered it was a limousine. The door behind the front passenger opened and I peered in. There I saw an identical man sitting inside. He didn't say anything, just looked directly in front of him. I felt afraid and walked off.

When I got home I was very shaken. The next day we saw an article in the Daily Mail *saying that Bobby Brown had been seen driving to Heathrow in a stretched limousine. We all thought it must have been him I saw playing a practical joke.*

The singer Bobby Brown had been in Leeds, 80 km (50 miles) north-west of Black Brook Farm. Laura did not actually see the singer – only three immaculately dressed men – and there is no reason why he would have been off the beaten track on his way to Heathrow Airport, 320 km (208 miles) south of the village. This episode illustrates the way the mind works when confronted with the bizarre. Contrary to what the sceptics would have people believe, the majority of percipients seek a rational, 'normal' explanation for their encounters. Many long to be told their experience was 'all in the mind'.

Throughout this book it has been stressed that UFO experiences should not be studied in isolation, but compared to other anomalous encounters. Here's another thread in the UFO web.

Laura Bond told us the following disturbing story of an incident that happened in October 1993:

I was standing at the bus-stop with Sonja waiting to go to the hospital. Just as the bus arrived a woman appeared and got on. I noticed her because of her extremely smart appearance and because she seemed to be watching Sonja. She sat down close to us and continued to look at her, but never smiled. I began to feel a little uneasy and felt she was listening to everything we were saying.

When we got off the bus she did the same and followed us into the café area of the hospital. After we had seen the doctor, I noticed she was still there, sitting in the same place. There was not even a coffee cup in front of her. It seemed she had no business in the hospital at all. She followed us back to the bus-stop and journeyed with us home. The woman got off one stop before ours.

I felt very nervous at the time, partly because of her appearance. She looked out of place in her bright-red dress with gold but-

tons. Her eyebrows were strange too, plucked to a moon shape. I thought she might be a child abductor.

Irrational? Since December 1990 police forces across the country have received hundreds of reports of callers presenting themselves as social workers or health carers. These bogus officials have turned up at houses and demanded to examine and take away children whom they claim are at risk. Often they have shown identity cards which are later discovered to be fake.

A typical case occurred on 10 October 1995. That morning Mark Dunn was alone in his home in Levenshulme, Manchester. His wife Lisa was out with their two children. Mark answered the door to a slim white woman aged around 35, of medium height. She had long dark curly hair, a thin face, nose and lips and prominent cheekbones. She was wearing round gold-rimmed glasses.

The woman told Mark she was from Manchester City Council social services and was investigating 'ill-treatment to the baby'. She stepped into the house and Mark asked for proof of identity. The woman said she would get it and walked over to a red late-model Ford Escort waiting outside with two men in it. Instead of returning, however, she climbed into the car and it sped off.

Peter Hough investigated a case which occurred in Leigh, Lancashire, on 6 December 1992. Mrs Carter, a community nurse, and her two young daughters were at home, but her husband, a self-employed mechanic, was working. At about 10.30 am Mrs Carter answered the door to a man in his early forties holding a clipboard. He was thinning on top, wore a moustache and had a scar on his right cheek. In what sounded like a Scottish accent, the man introduced himself as 'Albert Sutcliffe' and produced an identity card which displayed a photograph. Mrs Carter thought he said he was from either Adlington, or Accrington Social Services Department.

The visitor explained he was following up reports that Mrs Carter was not feeding her children a proper diet. At this point he called over a female colleague who was standing outside next to a silver Mercedes. As the woman walked up the short path, a large van with three women inside drew up beside the car. They all wore scarves, as did the first woman, who was now in the doorway. Mrs Carter noticed the words 'Child Protection' emblazoned on her scarf.

Mr Sutcliffe told her that the van was used to take away children at risk. In her case, however (having only just met Mrs Carter!), he had decided it would not be needed and he told his colleague to order the driver to leave. Then he requested that they be allowed inside the house. Bewildered and upset, Mrs Carter let them in.

The woman was in her early thirties and smartly dressed. She spoke very quickly, so it was often difficult to understand what she said. After checking the Carters' food cupboards they were shown upstairs, where the children were playing. Mr Sutcliffe asked if he could examine the six-year-old, but Mrs Carter refused and he accepted this. Back downstairs, he said she could keep his card because it had a contact telephone number on it. The woman then copied down some details from the girls' birth certificates.

As Mrs Carter stood up to make some coffee, Sutcliffe demanded the card back, as he wished to write something on the reverse. The card – crucial evidence – was never returned. After they had finished their drinks, the couple left. The visit had lasted approximately 45 minutes.

It was only when Mrs Carter told her husband about the visit that she realized something was very wrong. The police became involved. Local social services departments denied all knowledge of the pair. The police took away the birth certificates for fingerprinting and carried out door-to-door enquiries. Peter Hough talked to the Carters' neighbours but drew a blank, although one man thought he had seen the strangers' car cruising past the house since the visit.

Neither the Carters nor the authors have been told the results of the police investigation. With the Carters' permission, Hough wrote twice to the police but his letters were not even acknowledged.

Bogus social workers, or BSWs, like the MIB, play the role of officials and intimidate people. Sutcliffe was smartly dressed, but his scarred face seemed a deliberate part of the intimidation. Indeed, the name itself would frighten many women. Peter Sutcliffe, dubbed 'the Yorkshire Ripper', was the notorious killer of 13 women).

Like the MIB, BSWs sometimes behave in ways bordering on farce. Mrs Carolyn Beard answered her door in Ashton-under-Lyne to a woman claiming to be a social worker. The woman said she had seen Mrs Beard's toddler Jody eating a jam sandwich. In her opinion it was too late for the child to be eating and she had come to take her away. She made a grab for Jody and a desperate tug of war ensued as Mrs Beard struggled to hang on to her child. The BSW lost and walked away. The latest case involved the young son of murdered headteacher, Philip Lawrence. A man and a woman called at the house in December 1996 to take away the child for an examination. They left when his mother asked for identification.

Both the MIB and BSWs issue threats which they never actually carry out. To our knowledge there has been only one reported case of BSWs successfully abducting children. In this instance the boys involved were returned 45 minutes later and said that their abductors had simply taken them to a local park and bought them ice-cream. As Detective Superintendent Foss admitted, BSWs 'have had plenty of opportunity to abduct a child, but this has not happened.'

Throughout the investigation of such cases the police have been pressed by the media about the identity and motives of the visitors. At first senior officers speculated that they were dealing with 'a highly organized paedophile ring'. They also considered the idea that the visitors were thieves checking out houses for burglary. Then it was suggested that they were members of the Christian fundamentalist movement who wanted to examine children they suspected were being abused.

In fact, the police are as baffled as everyone else. After numerous investigations, not a single person has been arrested, even though the visitors arrive in broad daylight, often in distinctive vehicles.

The BSW phenomenon began shortly after the SRA scare and the Cleveland Affair of 1987, when 121 children in Cleveland, in the North of England, were taken from their parents, having been diagnosed as suffering from sexual abuse. The evidence came from two senior social workers: Dr Marietta Higgs and Dr Geoffrey Wyatt. Subsequently the 'evidence' was found to be badly flawed and most of the children were returned to their families.

These events changed the public perception of official child 'carers'. Many parents now viewed them as power-mad autocrats with a warped idea of what constitutes child abuse. Like the MIB, BSWs are a response to fear, created out of the despair that exists beneath the veneer of even the most stable societies.

Any remaining doubts that the MIB and BSWs are from the same source may be dispelled by a curious sequel to the case of Dr Hopkins. A few days after the incident at his house, Dr Hopkins' daughter-in-law Maureen received a telephone call from a man who claimed to know John, her husband. He asked if he and his female companion could visit them one evening. When Maureen told John about the call, he said he did not recognize the couple's names. He met them anyway, at a local restaurant, and brought them home for the evening.

The couple were in their mid-thirties, wore out-of-date clothes and behaved strangely. They walked with very short steps; the woman's legs seemed oddly jointed and her breasts hung to her waist. The pair lacked any social graces. After accepting drinks they did not touch them all evening. The man fondled his lady friend and asked if he was doing it right, then wanted to know if Maureen had any nude pictures of herself!

Eventually the couple decided to leave, but the man became paralysed; he was apparently losing 'energy'. His companion asked John to help her move him, but the man suddenly revived. They marched from the house in single file without saying goodbye.

The purpose of this display is unfathomable. Those researchers whose studies are confined to the MIB have no doubt as to their origins: their lack of social etiquette, unfamiliarity with normal household appliances and poor physical co-ordination suggest they are some sort of android robot, sent by the aliens to frighten off witnesses and investigators. The MIB draw attention to themselves, which is probably their intention.

Dark, sinister figures with supernatural abilities have been recorded throughout history and survive in folk tales. In the Elizabethan post-Reformation period, they were perceived as Satan or his attendant demons. In 1630, during the Great Plague of London, a man claimed to have been abducted by a dark stranger in a black carriage driven by black horses, a story which has echoes of Laura Bond's experience with the MIB in the black limousine.

The MIB and BSWs are every bit as real to the percipients as alien abductors are to their abductees. Indeed, in encounters with the former there is often more than one witness. Hallucination would seem to be an unlikely explanation. When the parallels with the BSWs are demonstrated, it is obvious that the MIB have nothing to do with extraterrestrials but everything to do with a root phenomenon that can manifest in any way it chooses.

Chapter 12

Hypnosis and False Memory Syndrome

There is a continuing debate regarding the use of hypnosis as a means of memory retrieval in UFO abduction cases. How reliable is subjects' recall under such circumstances? Do they accurately report what happened to them, or does hypnosis allow their imaginations free rein to create a false memory? Before we can even begin to answer such questions, we need to examine the very concept of 'mind'.

What is the mind, where does it reside and what are the effects of memory? These thoughts have puzzled man ever since he became aware that he was a thinking being. Does the mind exist apart from the physical brain and where does the mind store our memories? The ancient Greeks were the first systematically to record their conclusions about mind and memory, and Plato's theory of ideas formed the basis of an entire philosophical system, which continues to be a cornerstone of Western thinking.

In our own century, neuro-scientists have tried to formulate a physical theory of mind, identifying it with the chemical and mechanical processes of the brain. This is not a new idea, having its roots in the atomist theory of matter taught in the fifth century BC by the Greek philosopher Leucippus and his follower, Democritus.

There is a great polarization in the modern attitude to the subject. On the one hand is 'scientific' thinking and on the other common sense or 'naive realism'. In its extreme form, scientific thought identifies mind with brain, as merely a chemical process, while the common-sense school postulates that consciousness must exist apart from the physical brain – the mind which contemplates the brain must be something other than the brain. Neuro-science often finds the whole concept of consciousness a bit embarrassing, as it does not easily fit into a materialistic view of the working of the brain. Nor does memory, as a function of the mind, readily fit into simple scientific categories. The modern study of the unconscious began in the eighteenth century and continues to haunt our own.

The famous Canadian neuro-surgeon Wilder Penfield expanded the study of the brain by mapping areas of cerebral activity. By gently probing exposed brains during operations with lightly charged electrical rods, Penfield was able to establish areas of the physical brain where various thought processes take place and where certain types of memories appear to be stored. Yet, in the last of several definitive books he wrote on his researches, he admits that he did not see a scientific connection between the physical brain and the mind. Penfield concluded that neuro-science would never lead to a real explanation of mind or thought.

Sir John Eccles, an English neuro-surgeon and winner of the Nobel prize, and the philosopher Sir Karl Popper teamed up to write *The Self and Its Brain*, a modern restating of the theory of dualism, which maintains that the mind and body exist and work separately. As the human brain is the only known organ that actively contemplates itself and tries to understand its own working, it is little wonder that our self-contemplation is so incomplete and primitive. How can the self-contemplating rise above itself for an objective view?

In the eighteenth century, that wonderful 'Age of Enlightenment' when a great deal of original thinking took place, much time was spent on this subject, both in theory and in practice. Many physicians wanted to explore the mind–body relationship and its effect on disease. It has always been acknowledged that mental suffering can cause physical suffering too: a depressed state of mind can make us ill.

Until the latter half of the eighteenth century the only medical model available to the physician was that of the ancient Greeks. Other than that there was only a mystical belief in demonic possession dating from the Middle Ages. Then the German physician Franz Anton Mesmer arrived on the scene. He laid the foundations for the modern therapeutic use of hypnosis and for psychotherapy in general.

Mesmer believed that he was a channel for a mysterious 'fluid' which he could direct towards his patients, causing a violent crisis which rebalanced various physical and mental forces. Mesmer attributed his therapeutic successes to a physical agency he called 'animal magnetism' or 'mesmerism'. This 'magnetism' was later demonstrated to be the power of suggestion, which worked when the subject was in a state of trance.

A deepening of the hypnotic trance enabled it to be used to anaesthetize patients during medical procedures. Dr James Esdale of Scotland and Dr James Braid of Manchester so perfected the technique that they could amputate limbs and even carry out deep abdominal operations with little, if any, discomfort to the patient. The medical world opened its eyes.

The use of hypnosis for both entertainment on the stage and therapy in the hospital led to an exaggerated belief in its powers. A Dr Bernheim of Nancy in France became so convinced of the efficacy of suggestive therapy that he insisted that every patient entering his hospital should undergo at least one session. The 'father of neurology', Jean Martin Charcot, was head of a large teaching hospital in Paris, the Salpetrière, where Sigmund Freud was later to study. Each week he demonstrated to doctors and journalists that the symptoms of hysteria could be dramatically reproduced in the hypnotic trance.

The myths and legends which grew up around the hypnotic process culminated in the late-nineteenth-century novel *Trilby*, by George du Maurier, in which the evil Dr Svengali enslaves poor Trilby with hypnosis. The story is a good one, but a lot of the nonsense and inaccuracies about hypnosis which it spread have remained in the popular mind. The average sufferer who turns to hypnotherapy as a form of psychotherapy expects little short of a miracle. They assume that they will enter a deep sleep, during which they will be completely unaware, and awaken a changed person. However, as we have seen with some of our abductees, hypnosis can produce quite a dramatic reaction.

Consider the case of Sean Riley, an Irish featherweight boxer. Sean was 35 when he came to Moyshe Kalman for hypnotherapy. He was in his physical prime, but he was no longer boxing. In fact he had a menial job in the kitchen of a large industrial establishment in Doncaster. He was in such a state of despair and self-loathing that it is a wonder he was able to hold onto even this employment. Sean had never been married, but he was in a long-standing and stable relationship with an English woman. They had four children. Sean's problem was putting pressure on his personal relationships and making him desperate.

He seemed to have a completely irrational reaction to certain subjects and words. These caused him such distress that he was becoming withdrawn and reclusive. He could not bear to hear homosexuality or child abuse mentioned. Crude or slang expressions referring to these subjects were especially upsetting to him. If they were mentioned on the radio or television, Sean immediately had a severe panic attack. First he would become bright red and hot and sweat would pour from his face, back, chest and arms. Then his legs and arms would start to tremble, followed by a sharp pain in the left upper chest which travelled down his left arm, convincing poor Sean that he was having a massive heart attack.

The attacks became more frequent and violent and, although Sean told himself that the cause was only his mind, he could do nothing to lessen the effect. Sean began to withdraw socially. He knew that his reactions were abnormal and that something must be done before life became totally unbearable. While he and his partner could ill afford the cost of the therapy, he was determined to overcome his problem.

During Sean's first session he cried in great gulping sobs. For him, the humiliating factor was that he was unquestionably heterosexual and, like many provincial Irish men, of a truly gentle character. While he had enjoyed boxing, for him it was a sport – he hated violence – and although he did not have a hatred of homosexuals, as a Catholic, he felt that homosexuality was totally unnatural and sinful. Why should he, of all people, react so strongly to it?

Child abuse was a different matter. Sean utterly condemned the monsters who prey upon children and he could imagine himself using violence against such people. He spoke with pride of his children and felt he was a good father. He expected a miracle cure from hypnotherapy. He regarded hypnosis as a dangerous state from which he might very well not emerge intact, but believed it was worth taking the risk: his life had become unbearable.

The troubled boxer proved to be an excellent subject, entering into the somnambulant, or profoundly deep, hypnotic trance quickly and easily. Kalman explained that he did not use suggestion therapy or try to 'lead' his clients. In the first session he asked Sean to cast his mind back to childhood and begin to describe his thoughts. Sean's reaction was immediate and extremely violent. He propelled himself out of the reclining chair where he was lying onto the floor. Soon he was curled up in a tight ball, banging his head on the floor and screaming at the top of his voice. Kalman was used to grand abreactions (the reliving of trauma in therapy), but Sean's were the most violent he had witnessed.

Continuing to scream at full volume, Sean rolled fiercely about the room while Kalman, just barely ahead of him, moved potentially dangerous pieces of furniture out of his way. At last, stretched spread-eagled on his back, Sean lay with his head under the analyst's desk and his body sprawled out into the room. As he sobbed in a more subdued manner Kalman asked him what he was seeing. With another loud cry Sean attempted to sit up, breaking his nose on the underside of the desk and almost knocking himself out. With blood streaming from his nose and a face rapidly darkening into an enormous bruise, Sean – still deeply under hypnosis – began his story from beneath the desk.

In an agony of despair, he began to remember his childhood as a boarder in a famous remedial school on the West coast of Ireland run by a well-known teaching order of monks. Within a few days of his arrival, the monk who supervised the boys at bath time began to take an over-friendly interest in Sean. Brother Thomas would hug him in the shower and, in a pretence of applying soap, rub his hands all over the boy's body, openly manipulating his genitals. At first the innocent child was repelled by these attentions, but soon accepted them as a substitute for affection. Being away from home for the first time, Sean was no doubt in need of affection.

Not very long afterwards, Brother Thomas began to come into Sean's bedroom at night to tuck him in. One night the pats and hugs grew rougher and with little warning, he threw back the covers of Sean's little cot, pulled down his pyjamas, turned him over on his stomach and, stifling the boy's cries, sodomized him violently.

Sean was mortified and enraged by this first session of hypnotherapy. He had been totally unaware of any of these memories and found them hard to accept. The former boxer wept, with a great sense of relief, and begged Kalman to tell him whether the memories were 'true'. Sean began to feel very angry that he had been betrayed by his parents and the brothers. He went away in a daze of bewilderment.

Sean arrived early and eager for his second session, in which there was even more screaming and violence than in the first. Sean recalled trying in vain to repulse Brother Thomas, who was soon joined by one of his fellow monks with similar inclinations. As Sean relived his struggles of nearly 30 years earlier, he kicked out violently, begging his former attackers for mercy.

Sean appeared for his third session in an elated mood. He had not had a single panic attack in spite of situations which in the past would have been a strong stimulus. His partner had seen a dramatic change in his personality and he was feeling much better in general. At first Sean was a bit reluctant to regress. Then, suddenly, with a great howl of pain, he was back in his memories of abusive experiences in school.

Crying and sobbing like a very upset child, he recalled how, when he tried to get help to withstand his abusers, he found himself the victim of a large ring of older boys. Instead of being helped, he was gang-raped. Sean was incredulous; this hitherto repressed memory left him exhausted, weeping on the floor.

At the end of this session, Sean expressed his perplexity at forgetting such extraordinary things, but affirmed – as do most people who relive buried traumas – that suddenly many of the odd feelings and events in his life now made sense. Sean had taken up boxing in self-defence while at the school. His desire to attack physically those who had so viciously abused him and to make himself invulnerable was the motive behind his interest in the sport. As his memories came flooding back into his consciousness, Sean realized that the therapy had been successful. Two years after this brief analysis, he had a better job and he was happy at home with his family.

What can one make of the story of Sean? Had he uncovered the objective truth? Can the same question be asked about UFO abductees? Sean was certainly experiencing something that was important for him to describe. It changed his life for the better and helped him make more sense of his feelings. This happened to Janet, too (see Chapter 3). After her memories were exorcized, Janet's friends noticed that she was a happier, more relaxed young woman. She now had the confidence to change her job and move to the South of England.

FALSE MEMORY SYNDROME

For society in general, the healing recovery of repressed memories often poses a huge threat. The very belief in an unconscious mind frightens a lot of people. In addition, a growing number of outraged parents are protesting because they have been unjustly accused of criminal and deviant behaviour as the result of False Memory Syndrome (FMS).

FMS is seen as a phenomenon caused by gullible or unscrupulous therapists who plant stories in the minds of equally gullible or seriously unstable patients. Despite psychological studies which tend to show that it is very difficult to make people believe they have been abused, a large section of society takes comfort in the belief that FMS is widespread and the memories generated by therapy are unreliable and worthless. In both the USA and the UK distressed parents have formed organizations to spread awareness of FMS and combat the damage allegedly suffered by children who fall into the hands of misguided therapists.

During our work with abductees, we attempted on many occasions to encourage hypnotized subjects to invent stories, but without success. They stuck to accounts they believed to be true – even if they were undramatic – and did not make things up to 'please the hypnotist', as critics claim happens.

In the February 1996 issue of UK *Vogue*, the investigative journalist Linda Grant looks objectively at the issue and questions the motives behind the belief in FMS. She suspects that those who champion the theory are allowing women to continue to be victimized.

It has been argued by historians and scholars that Freud was one of the first men actually to listen to women and take seriously their stories of abuse. This resulted in his early 'seduction theory', which states that neurosis and hysteria are caused by the sexual abuse of children by family members or servants; the memories are repressed, only to be expressed later in sublimated forms. Freud later recanted and said that patients were either lying or cloaking their fantasies and taboo desires in vivid imagery. Freud's critics, however, maintain that his about-face was the result of pressure from the outraged medical and social establishment. Whatever the truth, today's supporters of FMS have taken up Freud's mantle. They insist that the supposed victims of childhood sexual abuse are either lying or expressing what they *want* to believe, attributing the blame to some guiltless family member.

In her *Vogue* article, Ms Grant describes how the FMS movement in the USA was founded after Jennifer Freyd, a professor of psychology, was accused by her mother of being 'mad' and the victim of false memories. Professor Freyd had accused her father of sexually abusing her. When the case became public, Peter Freyd, who was pleading his innocence, described a wonderful family home where all had been sweetness and light. Parents from all over the States rallied to his defence, shocked that anyone could believe the daughter's charges against this pillar of society. To the dismay of many, however, those who knew the family best sided with Jennifer. Peter Freyd's own brother unequivocally stated that his brother behaved in an inappropriate and highly sexual manner towards his daughter. In the UK, one of the greatest champions of FMS has been accused by both of his daughters of sexual abuse.

What does all this tell us about memory, its accuracy and meaning? How do we know whether what we remember really happened to us or not? How can a memory get 'lost'? For some light on this subject we turn to an American medical doctor, Lenore Terr.

Dr Terr is a psychiatrist whose original training was orientated toward a 'physical' or neuro-scientific approach to mental health. She is not part of the old psychoanalytical, memory-repression school which was once so popular in the USA. Her interest in false memory began with her highly original and exciting studies of traumatized children who had been the victims of kidnapping. While studying the effects of trauma on memory, Dr Terr was inspired to expand the horizons of her research to include adults and their struggle with recall and its effect on their lives. She addresses these issues in *Unchained Memories,* one of the most readable books on the subject.

Studies of both children and adults demonstrate that we can all be fooled to a high degree about what we have seen or thought we have seen. *However, few people can be fooled into believing that they have had an experience they did not in fact have.* This does not mean that two people who have the same experience will not interpret it very differently. Dr Terr concludes that we interpret our experiences dramatically and slowly incorporate our developed and coloured interpretations into what we believe to be accurate memories.

She tells the story of a famous singer who was sexually abused as a child. When an account of a private dispute with his manager was printed in the newspapers, the singer became insecure and began to be obsessed by his traumatic childhood experience.

At the time of the attack he had remembered a wealth of information which allowed the police to arrest and convict his abuser. However, he had felt exposed by the newspaper reports of the incident and left home to go away to school, where he was able to forget about his experience and carve out a life for himself. Now the renewed publicity made him feel exposed and vulnerable again. It was only when he went back to his home town and read the sensitive and discreet coverage the original story had received that he was able to dismiss the recurring thoughts which were disturbing him.

The memory he had created around his childhood trauma was highly innaccurate, but it still aroused in him strong feelings and reactions. The essential core of the memory was true: he had been attacked. He was not confused about the details of what had happened to him, but his beliefs about how much the neighbours knew, how many people were talking about him, were very inaccurate.

The Freudian theory of repression is – astonishingly – confirmed by Dr Terr's work. The principal goal of psychoanalysis is to achieve healing self-knowledge by overcoming repression. Modern clinical psychologists have often pointed out that, whereas some people seem to forget their traumas, some never forget them and others repress them. Having experimented with groups of children known to have suffered the trauma of being kidnapped and held by criminals, Dr Terr reaches a remarkable conclusion: children who regularly undergo traumatic or very unpleasant experiences develop an ability to 'hypnotize' themselves or switch off and bury such memories. The more terrible the trauma, the more complete the burial.

Dr Terr mentions the startling case of a former Miss America who suddenly announced to the world that she had remembered her father, an extremely respected community leader, repeatedly abusing her. When questioned, her sister also admitted suffering abuse but said she had never 'switched off'. Similarly, while some UFO percipients remember their experiences only under hypnosis, others appear to retain a full conscious memory of what happened to them.

It would seem that individuals who have endured repeated brutal, humiliating or dehumanizing traumas can spontaneously develop the ability to forget, suppressing distressing memories which threaten their ability to function normally, or even to carry on living. Evidence seems to indicate that *single* experiences of brutality, unless they are very painful or frightening, are rarely repressed. When the repressed memory surfaces, often the subject re-experiences much of the original pain. This reliving of the painful memory, abreaction, is often strenuously avoided by those undergoing therapy, just as they longed to escape the pain or shame of the actual event.

Sometimes the mind seems to play games of avoidance, utilizing phenomena such as 'screen memories'. These are false memories covering up real memories to hide the painful and unbearable truth. Abductees sometimes describe having seen playful rabbits or deer during a UFO experience. Some therapists believe these are an acceptable alternative to the ugly goblin-like creatures who were really there.

Mixing memory with fantasy can help sweeten the bitter pill of traumatic recall. Everyone who has listened to a radio phone-in programme is familiar with the person who calls with a dreadful personal problem, not for themselves, but for 'a friend'. The host may play along and discuss the 'friend's' problem, or challenge the caller to own up to having the problem themselves. In psychotherapy the same phenomenon occurs. It is easier to discuss terrible experiences if they happened to other people. So too it is easier to deal with guilty or shameful memories if all responsibility is transferred elsewhere, to 'extraterrestrials', for example.

When one reads Professor John Mack's remarkable book *Abduction,* it is very hard not to make this interpretation of a number of his cases. For instance, Mack tells the story of two teenage boys who spend the night together at the start of an exciting holiday, sleeping alone in the back of an estate car. Inevitably they start talking about sex and how they hope to lose their virginity during the holiday. When eventually they sleep one afterwards reports that he was abducted and forced to have sex with an alien female.

Mack seems to take the story at face value, but it is more likely that this was a misremembered wet dream or masturbation session, garbled through guilt or shame. This explanation makes more sense than the idea that beings from space used the youth in a hybrid-breeding programme. This does not mean that he is lying or trying to fool himself: his guilt prevents him from seeing clearly what actually happened. Like most 'false memories', this is a case of an incomplete or disguised memory.

That was the conclusion reached by Dr Alvin Lawson, a Californian lecturer in English, and the psychiatrist Dr William McCall, who carried out experiments in the late 1970s and early 1980s with subjects with no interest in or connection with UFO experiences. The subjects were hypnotized and then encouraged to invent an abduction experience. Their stories compared well with 'genuine' abduction accounts, although the experimenters did ask the hypnotized subjects leading questions. Nevertheless, there were differences. The subjects displayed no emotion or abreaction and doorway amnesia (see page 51) was absent from their accounts. Of more importance here was Lawson's and McCall's subsequent 'birth trauma' theory.

It has long been noticed how the Greys resemble the human foetus in appearance. Lawson and McCall developed this observation into a theory to explain abductions. They speculated that abductees were misremembering the trauma of birth, returning to their first experience of stress and distorting it into a memory of examination by aliens. It seems unlikely that newborn babies are capable of retaining memories of their birth. Even if they were, it would take a great leap in logic to accept that the birth imagery could later take on fantastic dimensions. However, there is evidence that people can 'customize' unpleasant memories.

In *Unchained Memories* Dr Terr tells the revealing story of a girl who became antagonistic towards her family, especially her mother, when she began to remember being abused by her grandfather, to whom she had been particularly close. It transpired that the girl's mother had taken her for a particularly painful and frightening bladder examination and the doctor had looked remarkably like her grandfather: not a false, but an inaccurate memory.

In approaching the thorny subject of the 'truth' of memories, one should always bear in mind the fact that all memories mean something. Before dismissing a 'false memory' simply as false – the girl was not abused by her relative, the teenage boy was not abducted and seduced by aliens – we must ask what significance the memory has for the individual concerned. To dismiss masses of evidence that thousands – possibly millions – of people are remembering *something* seems unwise. The wise researcher will try to discover just *what* they are really remembering.

Chapter 13

Mind Games

What kind of people have UFO abduction experiences? Studies show that abductees are people like you – or your neighbour, best friend, husband, wife, girlfriend or boyfriend. They are not generally drunks, drug addicts, mentally handicapped people or pathological liars, although these also have such experiences, just as they share human experience in general.

The late Ken Phillips, a researcher who worked for many years with psychologist Dr Alex Keul, examined the life profiles of close-encounter percipients. At the end of the Anamnesis Project, as it was called, they concluded that percipients are normal, healthy individuals from a cross-section of society. However, there was a greater tendency towards claims of ESP compared with the researchers' control sample.

Studies by American researchers show that as many as 3.7 million adults in the USA fit a profile associated with extraterrestrial contact. The psychologists Professor Leo Sprinkle and June Parnell studied over 200 subjects who believed they had been in contact with aliens. The results were presented in their paper, 'Personality Characteristics of UFO Witnesses', published in 1986. None of the 'contactees' were found to be mentally ill. Our observations concur with this finding. However, the researchers Eric Jacobson and Joanne Bruno, who examined twelve abductees, discovered that two of them met the criteria for major psychiatric disorders.

Some sceptics have argued that percipients of anomalous phenomena have a 'fantasy-prone personality' or FPP, that they are so immersed in make-believe that they cannot tell it apart from reality. This condition is epitomized in the legendary Karl Friedrich, Freiherr von Münchhausen. He was a character so caught up in fantasy that he lost sight of truth and began to live partly in his imagination. The original von Münchhausen was a minor nobleman and soldier who, like the old soldiers of fireside lore, told his stories so often and enlarged upon them so regularly that the line between truth and dreams was blurred. Is he lying, enjoying a flight of fantasy, can he tell the difference after doing it year upon year?

Take the case of Dr K.M., a young GP. One evening after an exhausting spate of home visits he called on Moyshe Kalman for a shot of his favourite single malt. He had intended to stay for ten minutes, but as the two began to swap strange case histories, the scotch flowed and time flew. After an hour and a half he sprang to his feet and rushed to the telephone to call his wife, who was stuck at home with six small children.

'Sorry I'm late, dear,' he said, 'but I'm at North Manchester General. I've had to section a dangerous psychopath. I'm okay, but it was very messy. Be home in about 30 minutes.'

Kalman was amazed to hear his friend tell such a tall tale, and asked him if he really had sectioned a psychopath that evening.

'Why do you ask?,' replied the doctor.

'Well, you just told your wife you did, didn't you?'

'Oh, did I? I really don't remember.'

This odd conversation led to a discussion of memory and truth, during which Dr K.M. freely admitted that, given the choice, he would always tell a lie instead of the truth. He added that he lies so often, especially to his wife, that he is rarely even aware of it. His memory is excellent and seems to work on 'automatic pilot', switching to lying mode without effort and maintaining the consistency of his stories.

Can day-dreaming, which is a sort of lying to yourself, become so much a part of life that it becomes reality for some people? From a psychological perspective, what is happening in the life of the fantasy-prone individual? Is fantasy an attempt to shield oneself from unpleasant facts such as the consequences of one's errors, or is it a safety-valve that allows the (perhaps bored and frustrated) personality to achieve wish-fulfilment? Maybe it is a combination of the two. We all laugh at poor Walter Mitty, but in our hearts we know what he is experiencing.

In the USA, some well-known psychologists have tried to study the FPP. The first to write about this type of personality were Theodore X. Barber and Sheryl C. Wilson. Their work and the work of others in this field was described and evaluated at the Abduction Study Conference held at the Massachusetts Institute of Technology (MIT) in June 1992. An Australian UFO investigator, Keith Basterfield, noted that all the members of the first group of FPPs to be studied were women who had some remarkable things in common.

Over half had experienced false pregnancies; some had even tried to have abortions. More than half felt that, while fantasizing, even with eyes wide open they could not tell the difference between fantasy and objective reality. The mind of the FPP seems to be directed by his or her fantasies, rather than the other way around. Three-quarters of the women were able to achieve orgasm through fantasy alone. On the whole these FPPs lived in a childhood world of fairies and fantasy beings and often had imaginary friends and companions; most had an excellent memory, especially about childhood.

It is not hard to see how the sceptic could easily explain away most, if not all, abductions in terms of FPP. Several of the percipients we interviewed appear, on the surface at least, to match the description of the FPP. If your fantasies are as real to you as reality, you might easily slip into 'abduction mode'.

Basterfield cites two studies of abductees in which the researchers looked for the FPP factor. Both studies concluded that the typical abductee was not a FPP, but one concluded that the FPP and the abductee did have certain characteristics in common. They shared a rich inner life of thought, looking for meaning beyond the obvious and below the surface of things. Both groups were said to have 'a degree of identity disturbance' and to be always 'looking for an identity', seeking to define themselves in relation to the world around them. They were reported to have minor problems with personal relationships and to be slightly paranoid.

These particular personality factors can often be observed in people who believe they have been abducted or contacted by aliens. They are all present in Dr K.M. as well, although, as far as we know, he has never been abducted. He tries to avoid relations with his wife and admits to a rich erotic fantasy life revolving round his female patients. Having a very high IQ, he was able to do well at school without effort and whiled away long, dull hours in fantasy.

The habit has become difficult to break.

Mark Rodeghier, Scientific Director for the Centre for UFO Studies, presented some test results to the 1992 MIT conference. A sample of 32 abductees were given an ICMI (Childhood Memory and Imagination) test. The scale runs from zero to 52. The mean score was 24, which compares well with the general population (between 20 and 24). Only two of those tested registered high enough scores to be classified as fantasy-prone.

In his concluding remarks at the conference, Basterfield observed that, while the FPP type makes up only about 4 per cent of the population, and in no way accounts for the bulk of the abductee phenomenon, it does have a central role to play.

Chapter 14

The Sacred
Sickness

The holy man, dressed in a ragged toga, shambled out of the temple to talk to the crowd who waited to see him. His hair was flecked with bits of straw and feathers and his face, slightly swollen from sleep, had the vacant air of someone who was either distracted by higher thoughts or simply a fool.

The wealthy farmers had travelled from remote areas of Greece. They were worried about a continuing pestilence in the olive groves which threatened yet another year's crops. They pressed around the holy man, who seemed hardly to notice their urgent questions and prayers for blessings. The two accompanying priests with their ceremonial wands exuded an air of dignity which kept the desperate countrymen from actually touching the holy man or tugging at his robe to attract his attention. They were engaged in a familiar ritual which they had repeated many, many times.

At a clearing near the edge of the market the potter had prepared his wheel. The large turntable, powered by the potter's feet, glistened with slip, the thin clay mixture used to cement together complex pots and lubricate the surface of the clay while the pots were thrown. This morning the potter would not be shaping pottery vessels, but helping to mould the destiny of his fellow creatures in an ancient ritual he knew as well as the solemn priests.

The potter began to spin his wheel. The shining disc rotated faster and faster, throwing bits of slip onto the fine robes of the unconcerned priests; the more practical farmers backed a short distance away. When the wheel became a blur of shimmering wetness, the older of the two priests nodded to the potter, who slowly poured a small jug of water over its surface. The younger priest gently, almost lovingly, held the holy man's face between crown and chin and guided it so that he looked at the shining disc. Within seconds his eyes began to roll upwards, exposing the bloodshot whites, and his head began to tremble. The farmers involuntarily took a few more steps back, trembling with awe. With a terrible scream the holy man threw up his left arm and struck himself violently in the face. His whole body now jerked in a massive contortion and as he fell on his back his bladder and bowels emptied forcefully.

Lying facing up into the hazy sky with unseeing eyes, the holy man began to groan. A thin line of blood issued from the left corner of his mouth where he had bit his tongue. The priests eagerly fell to their knees in reverence, straining to catch his sacred utterances. The elder whispered questions in the holy man's ear and he began to jabber. An incoherent babble poured from his mouth, as foolish-sounding as the talk of foreign merchants from far-off Phoenicia or Persia, occasionally interspersed with a recognizable word. 'Olive' was heard several times, giving the frightened farmers hope, despite their horror at what they were witnessing. The priests eagerly listened to each sound and the younger one recorded the most obscure in mysterious symbols scratched on a shard of broken pottery, lest they be forgotten.

In a few minutes the holy man began to revive. He blinked his eyes in the painfully bright light and struggled unsteadily to sit up. The farmers roused themselves from their fear and rushed to help him to his feet. Then the older priest examined the bitten tongue and, satisfied that the injury was not serious, began to direct the party back toward the temple. The holy man returned to his pallet of straw in a dark corner of the building, while the priests retired alone to interpret the message he had given them from the gods. When they returned, the farmers were overjoyed to learn that fortune was now smiling on them. They were instructed to sacrifice a fine fat sheep and to spend the night in the temple and await a holy dream. Then they would be free to return to their fields and orchards; there would be a good harvest this year.

Not just in Greece, but all over the ancient world this scene was acted out again and again. Then one voice questioned the meaning of the ritual. Hippocrates suggested that the holy men's 'sacred illness' or 'falling sickness' was due to a physical abnormality of the brain and not the action of the gods. With this impious observation the modern understanding and treatment of epilepsy began.

The fact that almost every culture in the world has viewed epilepsy as something special, either a blessing or a curse, rather than a disease made the objective study of this unique condition very difficult. The major medical breakthrough came in the late nineteenth century when the father of British Neurology, Dr J. Hughlings Jackson, turned his attention to the subject and carried out some very famous experiments. In a time when animal experimentation was still an accepted part of medical research, Jackson was able to demonstrate the links between certain areas of the brain and involuntary muscular reactions. Applying his results to the symptoms of epilepsy, he was able to define two major types of seizure: Primary or Generalized and Focal or Partial.

Of all neurological conditions, epilepsy is probably the most common. Some specialists claim that almost 10 per cent of the population experience at least one seizure in their life. Probably as much as 4 per cent of the population will have a tendency to seizures during a particular period of their lives, such as adolescence, while about 0.5 per cent of the general population will remain prone to regular attacks.

Most people are aware only of the Primary form of epilepsy because of its dramatic manifestations. While the vast majority of epileptic seizures are of very short duration and harmless, the *grand mal* fit of Primary epilepsy will never be forgotten once witnessed. It often strikes without warning and the victim suffers a generalized electrical brain discharge which leaves him or her unconscious and convulsing. The whole experience may be over almost as fast as it began, or it could last for several minutes. The danger of injury comes mainly from the fall which the unconscious sufferer sustains. Modern medication to limit and control the discharge now enables most sufferers to lead normal lives.

The Focal type of epilepsy is less well known to the general public, but far more widespread. The most common form of focal seizure (a seizure which originates at a single focal point in the brain or which remains focused in one area rather than spreading or generalizing) is known as Temporal Lobe Epilepsy (TLE). Here, the electrical discharge remains in the temporal lobe of the brain. This form of epilepsy has a whole host of complex and subtle characteristics which are often mistaken for other conditions.

In many cases of TLE the episode or fit begins with an 'aura' or feeling which the sufferer learns to recognize. This may be a smell (mostly of something burning), a strange taste, a feeling of dizziness or just a sensation that is impossible to describe. The entire fit is often limited to this aura and the strange taste or smell is believed to be external and objectively 'real', so that other possibilities are never investigated. In the past, people who continually complained of strange aromas no one else could smell, or noticed an inexplicable odd taste in the mouth, were thought to be mad.

The aura of the attack may also have a strong emotional content: sufferers may experience extreme but irrational fear or anxiety which makes them appear to be paranoid. There are cases in which the aura is composed of strong feelings of having been somewhere before, resulting in a powerful *déjà vu* experience.

In a minority of cases, there are other characteristics which are relevant to the subject of alien abductions and UFO encounters. Many TLE sufferers experience auditory and visual hallucinations and because, unlike the victims of Primary epilepsy, they do not become unconscious, their illusions seem quite real and they may find it very hard to believe they are not. It is easy to see why epileptics were often viewed as shamen or holy men – men of visions.

Perhaps the most remarkable phenomenon associated with this particular form of epilepsy is the epileptic fugue or dissociation of the personality. In some cases, when the actual fit seems to be over, the victim is left in a fugue, a state of mental confusion. In this state he will often not know where he is or what he is doing, and often wanders away or even boards a train or plane, only to find himself completely lost later on. Many people have been demonstrated to be highly suggestible while in fugue. Commands or instructions given to the victim are often carried out unquestioningly and this can lead to extraordinary situations.

As we saw in our recreation of augury by an epileptic 'holy man' in ancient Greece, the fit can be induced by spinning shining objects like the shining, wet potter's wheel. The easiest way to induce a fit is to have the sufferer stare at alternating or flickering light. A candle can be an excellent stimulus and it is interesting that candles play a part in occult rituals. Stroboscopic lighting in a disco, which often provokes epileptic episodes in people not previously known to have a tendency to the condition, is another stimulus, as is the swinging watch of the hypnotist. In the early days of the cinema, when the picture flickered the flickering screen was often enough to induce a fit; the cinema is still sometimes referred to as 'the flicks'. If a suggestive fugue resulted, victims were often left trying to act out the scenes of the film which had become imprinted on their minds. They fully believed they had personally experienced what they had in fact only seen on the screen.

In a celebrated case in the USA a man regularly arrived at work in the mornings in a fugue state, not knowing where he was and often trying to act out strange scenes which he felt were important but which appeared out of place in his life. This caused such problems at his place of employment that a thorough investigation was carried out, with remarkable conclusions.

The man in question always travelled to work on the same bus, usually sitting on the same side. It was noted that the fugue happened only on sunny days and that at one point on the bus route, our victim was subjected to the sun shining on a picket fence (a white open-work fence of narrow upright posts). On bright, sunny days the sun on the fence created the perfect pattern to send the man into a TLE fit, resulting in a fugue state. His bizarre behaviour seemed to be motivated by suggestions he had picked up from conversations overheard on the bus or bits of radio programmes he had been listening to on his Walkman. The strange problem never occurred again when the man took care not to look at the fence!

In one of the most remarkable yet little publicized books on the subject, *Hypnotism, Hysteria and Epilepsy*, by E.M. Thornton, the author makes an excellent case for all the trappings of hypnotism associated with the stage – apparent unconsciousness, post-hypnotic suggestibility, fugue and the implantation of false beliefs – being part and parcel of TLE fits. Any professional hypnotist will confirm that some people make better subjects than others: They 'go deeper' than others and are more open to suggestion.

After years of hypnotizing patients for various purposes, Moyshe Kalman can affirm that there are definitely two phenomena known as 'hypnotism' which appear to be similar but are probably unrelated. The most common and most useful for therapeutic purposes is a deeply relaxed and undistracted state in which memory is enhanced and so concentrated that patients are able to 'look within' to a greater degree than usual. In this state they experience both memory and remembered emotion more acutely. This type of hypnotic focusing, directed by a skilful therapist, is available to almost every person over the age of four who is sober and of unimpaired intellect. This is also an ideal state of mind for dynamic psychotherapy; the hypnotized subject can more easily recall important lost memories, feel them deeply and remember the contents of the session later on and reflect on them.

The second state is more like the condition the stage hypnotist achieves and involves amnesia, extraordinary fantasy and extreme suggestibility. This type of hypnosis is a state of mind that almost everyone fears when first visiting a hypnotherapist. 'Will I remember what I said?' and 'Will I do silly things?' are questions almost always asked. In fact, this state of mind is practically useless for therapy.

Consider the case of Ellen N. A very large lady in her late thirties who looked at least 50, Ellen was diabetic and found it impossible to control her food intake, hence her size. She had recently been divorced after an abusive marriage and had an uncontrollable sweating problem. She was a very intelligent woman with a charming personality, but she seemed on the verge of being overwhelmed by her condition. She came to Moyshe Kalman for treatment because of a phobia of needles, sharp objects and penetration. About a year earlier she had undergone an operation for her sweating problem which was partially successful. The second stage of the operation could not take place because of Ellen's violent reactions during the first. When she was given an injection to prepare her for the operation, Ellen had succeeded in injuring several nurses and, although a mild-mannered lady, had used such foul language that the hospital staff refused to continue the treatment.

As if this situation was not bad enough, Ellen was having greater and greater difficulties with her diabetes. She ate constantly and consumed large quantities of sweet foods. Her doctor informed her that the problem was becoming so severe that the stimulating tablets she now took would soon be inadequate; she would eventually have to inject herself with insulin. The thought of the injections was too much and Ellen decided to seek therapy.

She was absolutely terrified of hypnosis, but less terrified than she was of needles. Kalman did his best to convince her that she would simply relax and begin to slip back into her memories as they tried to find out why she reacted so strongly to needles. Ellen made the therapist swear that she would not be forced to touch or fantasize about needles.

She settled in a soft chair with obvious fear and Kalman approached with a Babinsky hammer, a chrome disc on a long handle used to test knee-jerk reflexes. He held the disc just above Ellen's line of vision and asked her to stare at it as he rotated the long handle, causing the shining disc to turn back and forth. Ellen's body jerked violently in the chair, her eyes rolled upward and she slumped down, almost falling onto the floor. Her head lolled over the arm of the chair and she began to beg the therapist to 'release' her. Kalman reassured Ellen that she was safe and exercising total self-control. Eventually she started to calm down, although she continued to throw her huge bulk from side to side as though she were struggling to free herself from some invisible bonds.

Ellen refused point-blank to free associate in order to uncover repressed or forgotten memories. The therapist, seeing that Ellen was a good or 'deep-trance' subject, decided to do something rather radical. He assumed a commanding tone and ordered Ellen to return to the memories responsible for her presenting problem. She immediately assumed a child-like voice and begged not to be forced to tell 'what happened'. The therapist insisted. With great sobs and screams Ellen described her mother violently forcing the nozzle of an enema syringe into her anus and then sadistically using a similar instrument to inflict painful vaginal douching. These 'memories' puzzled Moyshe Kalman as he knew Ellen's mother well; a tiny, cowering Eastern European refugee, she seemed to dote on her ungainly daughter. Ellen accompanied her account with shouts and screams of pain, all the while pleading for mercy and not to be forced to remember.

With great difficulty Kalman brought Ellen out of her trance. Usually subjects return to the non-trance state after a simple suggestion. Ellen was reluctant and seemed unable to come back to a state of full comprehension for quite some time. She was confused for a few minutes and then asked very sweetly if hypnosis was going to be used or not. To the amazement of the therapist, Ellen remembered nothing at all about the session and refused to believe that she had been hypnotized. Afraid that telling Ellen the nature of her memories would probably cause them to become more deeply repressed, Kalman refused to discuss her revelations. He instructed her to return home, try to relax and remember what she had said.

At the next session Kalman induced, with great ease, a very deep trance. Ellen was again taken, under protest, back to the experiences she had remembered. This time she was ordered to recall them in detail when the trance ended. At the close of this session her fugue state was more profound and Ellen remembered absolutely nothing of what she had said. She also felt that her phobias were becoming worse.

This was repeated five times until Kalman had the idea of recording the session and allowing Ellen to hear herself afterwards. Ellen refused to listen to the recording in his presence and took the tape home. When she returned she still had not been brave enough to listen to it and mentioned that she was in great pain from bleeding piles, but, of course, could not go for treatment because of her phobias. As this session ended Kalman repeated several times a strong suggestion that Ellen would, without thinking about it, leave the consulting room, go to the local hospital and demand to have her piles injected. Ellen stood up on command and left without making another appointment or saying goodbye. She telephoned later the next day, asked for an immediate appointment and arrived with a black eye!

'I don't know what came over me. I left here, though I don't remember it, and went to the hospital, demanding treatment,' Ellen told the therapist. When the staff saw the dangerous state of the bleeding, they attempted to begin emergency treatment. A battle royal ensued, resulting in several injuries to the staff and Ellen had been given a police caution, but her piles were injected! Kalman was shocked to realize the extent of the danger to which he had subjected his patient: sent away in a fugue condition, she had submitted to minor surgery against her will and inflicted physical harm on the hospital staff.

At one level Ellen was very open to post-hypnotic suggestion, but resisted the suggestion consciously to remember what she recalled under hypnosis. As she was brought out of hypnosis again, while still in her confused, fugue state, she dreamily listened to the recording of her ordeal. The tears flowed freely and Ellen began the process of consciously remembering her childhood, though at first she refused to believe that it was really her speaking on the tapes.

In a rage she confronted her mother and the old lady admitted that what Ellen had remembered was accurate, but said she had only been trying to help her. Ellen's anger eventually receded and she began to lead a normal life. What had happened during the hypnosis process? The therapist had unknowingly induced a TLE seizure.

It is impossible to ignore the parallels between this case and that of Betty and Barney Hill (see plate section). The Hills' was one of the first 'classic' cases of UFO abduction extensively to be investigated in the USA. Betty and Barney were able to enter the hypnotic trance state which left little conscious memory afterwards. Their memories were not 'healing' ones; they had no catharsis from the hypnotic experience. They were amazed and troubled by hearing the tapes of their memories, but coming to terms with some of the contents of the memories eventually seemed to have a positive effect. If this indicates that the Hills were suffering from TLE, does it automatically follow that their condition was responsible for the alleged abduction experience, as some critics believe?

Barney, a black American who was married to a white woman at a time when, even in enlightened New England, mixed marriages were unusual, had an understandable fear of being persecuted. He recalled a time when he was particularly vulnerable: while he was swimming in a river, he and his son were 'buzzed' by a plane – an experience he took very personally. The Hills claimed to have been abducted on a flight back from Canada on the night of 19 September 1961. During the journey, Barney had felt very threatened by some rough-looking youths. Betty was very interested in flying saucers. Her sister had claimed to have spotted one and Betty was excited about this and perhaps just a bit jealous. Who knows what really happened on that night? The results of the Hills' hypnosis sessions do sound like the fugue state of an epileptic fit mixed with genuine fears expressed in the language of science fiction.

The case is a highly complex one, however, and this explanation may be too simplistic. Betty described an unusual medical procedure carried out on her by the aliens which was connected, she was told, with pregnancy testing. A few years later, exactly the same procedure was used to test for Down's Syndrome. There was evidence that something inexplicable was in the area that night, too:

an object was tracked on radar by a local Air Force base. There are similarities between the Hills' case and Ellen's case, and what she remembered was later verified as being factually accurate. Ellen did not dress up the enema episodes as Satanic ritual abuse or part of an alien abduction experience.

Some fairly convincing attempts have been made to find a mechanism that might affect the brain, trigger off TLE and produce hallucinations. As we have seen, rapid flickering lights can be responsible for epileptic attacks. Is it a coincidence that witnesses often describe UFOs as pulsating, or possessing patterns of flickering lights? Perhaps UFOs are objectively real but abduction experiences are a consequence of the space crafts' pulsating light patterns, which cause hallucinations in people prone to TLE.

Reports of 'earthquake lights' were reported, and ignored by scientists, for years. It was not until 1910 that the phenomenon was taken seriously. The effects consisted of balls or aurora-like displays of light in the atmosphere before or just after an earthquake. Modern research indicates that similar phenomena can occur over fault lines at times of seismic stress. The Chinati Mountains near Marfa in Texas and the Pennines in the North of England are examples of heavily faulted areas where unexplained lights have often been recorded, photographed and filmed.

Popular attention was drawn to the subject in 1977 by the Canadian researchers Michael Persinger and Gyslaine Lafrenière when they published *Space-Time Transients and Unusual Events*. Persinger is professor of psychology and research science, and head of the Neuroscience Laboratory at Laurentian University in Sudbury, Ontario. In 1982 Paul Devereux, a researcher, and Paul McCartney, a geochemist, published *Earth Lights*, which drew together various aspects of the subject and presented new regional studies.

These researchers postulate that seismic stress deep beneath the Earth's crust can cause electrically charged plasma to manifest in the air above fault lines. The mechanism for this is called the 'piezo-electric effect'. It is postulated that quartz crystal-bearing rock put under tremendous pressure would release the plasma. Laboratory experiments by Persinger produced small electrical charges. In recent years the principle has been adapted to develop lighters for domestic gas appliances.

Researchers believe not only that aerial plasma balls would be interpreted as UFOs by distant observers, but that anyone in close proximity would be directly affected as the electrical field of the light form interacted with the observer's brain. Devereux, who had personally experienced the phenomenon, speculated that an empathy with the brain would produce a structural change in the plasma ball itself. An observer who thought 'UFO' would draw the appropriate imagery from his subconscious, and a signal would be sent to the plasma, which would then represent the thought visually. There have been many accounts of unusual mists or clouds changing into solid-looking flying-machines.

Persinger has kept his extrapolations within acceptable scientific boundaries. He postulates that electromagnetic fields emanating from the phenomenon would affect the temporal lobe area of the brain and causes close-encounter hallucinations.

Dr M.C. Walker, Research Fellow in the Epilepsy Research Group at the Institute of Neurology in England, does not agree. He states that the magnetic fields used in research to stimulate the brain are over 10 000 times greater than the Earth's magnetic field. Such high magnetic fields are not reproduced as a result of earthquake activity and, he asserts, there is no evidence that some people's brains are 10 000 times more sensitive than others. Although not a believer in UFOs, Dr Walker concludes that, given a choice between Persinger's theory and the effects being caused by UFO activity, he would back the UFOs.

In 1995 the ufologist Albert Budden published *UFOs: Psychic Close Encounters*. This book was Budden's attempt to take the work of Persinger and Devereux a step further. He postulated that artificial electromagnetic pollution was interacting with witnesses' brains and causing or allowing the unconscious to create dramatically staged events. These events are not 'all in the mind' but have an objective reality. Budden states:

It is the activity of the human unconscious in combination with a variety of natural and artificial energies that produces staged realities identified as the close-encounter experience. It is the unconscious – or, more descriptively, the unconscious intelligence – that utilizes its reality-defying abilities (including psychokinesis or 'mind over matter') to produce the effects of an advanced, mag-

ical technology in these 'staged productions', its motivating purpose being to establish and maintain an external social identity.

He questions the entire concept of reality and compares the unconscious to a genie corked up in a bottle. Trapped, it can only subtly influence reality, but when an interaction with electromagnetic pollution occurs, the genie is released to work its magic. Its raw materials are the images of folklore, the occult and science fiction stored in the memory banks of the brain.

Budden believes that some people are more susceptible than others to the effects of electromagnetic fields. He refers to it as an 'allergy' and, as with other allergies, there are varying conditions of resistance.

In his study Budden has re-examined various cases, looking for sources of electromagnetic pollution such as fault lines, radio wave-transmitting antennae, microwave towers, television masts and high-tension electrical cables. 'Places of power', paranormal 'hot spots' or 'window areas' are locations, he argues, where there is a lethal combination of natural and artificial radiation. Budden has been very successful in discovering such sources.

He might be interested to learn that along the railway embankment close to Black Brook Farm runs a high-tension power cable. This was erected a year after the Bonds moved in and before their spectacular UFO encounter. However, critics will argue that it would be difficult *not* to find some electromagnetic pollution at the scene of an abduction or close-encounter experience. In the Bonds' case, as we have seen, the effects continue, even though the three daughters have moved away from the farm.

Budden stresses the importance of temporal lobe stimulation with regard to 'visitor' experiences, and quotes Persinger:

Such experiences are thought to be correlated with mesobasal (amygdaloid hippocampal) portions of the temporal lobes. These areas of the brain are associated inter alia with the experience of meaningfulness, the sense of self and its relationship to space-time (with its religious or 'cosmic' associations), fear, dreams, experiences of movements (like spinning or floating), smell and memory storage and retrieval. Consequently, there should be (and there are) references to the sense of presence, feelings of spinning or floating, or of vibrations; dreamlike sequences; and fear or irri-tability.

In a BBC *Horizon* documentary which critically examined the UFO abduction phenomenon, Professor Persinger attempted to induce TLE in the psychologist Dr Sue Blackmore. Blackmore has been a vociferous champion of TLE as a cure-all for paranormal ailments.

For the experiment Dr Blackmore put on a helmet wired up to equipment which sent pulses of electromagnetic energy into the temporal lobes of her brain. At one point she became quite excited and explained that she could feel a hand on her leg. Unfortunately, she did not experience the highly complex scenario of being abducted and examined by aliens. Nor did she describe seeing a ghost, or meeting a sinister Man in Black.

Dr Walker explained the reasons for this failure in a letter to the ufologist Harry Harris: although brain stimulation has induced effects like limb movements, illusions of light, fear and depersonal-ization, it has never induced complex, prolonged hallucinations.

Chapter 15

Under Examination

I f close-encounter subjects are prone to temporal lobe epilepsy there should be some evidence for it. Unfortunately there has not been any wholesale testing of abductees. One of the first to be tested, however, was Whitley Strieber (see plate section).

After his abduction experience on 26 December 1985, Strieber thought he had a mental problem and sought the help of a number of different doctors. He underwent tests by two different neurologists and, according to him, neither could find any evidence of brain abnormality. It was Dr Donald Klein who suggested Strieber might be suffering from temporal lobe epilepsy.

Strieber subjected himself to painful laboratory tests and reportedly came out with a clean bill of health. In Strieber's book, *Communion*, Dr Klein states: 'he is not suffering from any psychosis'. The UFO debunker Philip Klass takes issue with this in his book, *UFO Abductions: A Dangerous Game*.

In his second book, *Transformation,* Strieber maintains that all the medical records of his tests were handed over to Dr John Gliedman, who was given permission to discuss the findings with inquirers who have medical and scientific credentials. When Klass tried to gain access to the records it was denied. Klass finds this very suspicious, but Strieber probably fears that Klass, an aviation journalist, might selectively quote from the material to support his anti-UFO stance.

As we read in Chapter 3, when Janet was tested the doctors could not find any kind of brain abnormality. Fortunately Laura Bond, one of the women from Black Brook Farm,was determined to find a scientific explanation for her experiences and sought medical help.

She was tested for TLE. This is how her mother described one of Laura's 'attacks', which occurred while she was a teenager:

One of the worst things that happened was when Laura had a strange reaction during a particularly stressful time. It occurred one evening while we were having a discussion. Laura was dozing when she became very distressed, clutching at the air, unaware of her surroundings. We took her outside and tried to bring her round. The doctor attended. Afterwards she was suffering from shock. She felt she had been dragged downwards through a brightly lit tunnel, and referred to a 'sinking feeling'. This happened at other times to a lesser degree whilst she was falling asleep.

Laura's attack was diagnosed as a form of epilepsy. However, some years later when she was married and expecting a baby, she took herself off the medication and is fine now. I wonder, and so does she, if it really was epilepsy.

The discussion the family had been having concerned the incidents at the farm and how they were getting out of hand. Not only Laura and her mother, but also her doctors, had doubts about the diagnosis, as we discovered when we examined her medical records. During our investigation of the case, and after Joyce had made the above statement to us, Laura pursued her quest to find a medical explanation for her experiences. She felt that this would be easier to accept than the alternative: that she was the victim of some sinister outside force. This is what she told us in September 1993:

I'm trying to think of ways to stop it happening. I'm seeing a neuro-psychiatrist soon and maybe he'll diagnose epilepsy or sleep paralysis. Then I can take drugs to prevent it. Perhaps it's an evil spirit like an incubus feeding off my negative thoughts. In which case I'll start going to church. My worst fear is that its an alien abduction, and then there's absolutely nothing I can do.

Laura listed six stages of her attacks:

1. Usually something wakes her up, a child crying, her name being called or an itchy ear.

2. The sinking feeling takes hold. It comes in waves and she tries to fight it, but sometimes it is too strong.
3. Paralysis slowly overcomes her. She tries very hard to move, but the effort required is too great. She cannot move her eyes or even make a noise. Now she feels totally numb and finds it increasingly hard to fight off the sinking feeling.
4. She has only had this stage once. It was the most frightening thing that has ever happened to her. The instant she stopped fighting she shot off at a great speed. It was like being on a roller-coaster, bright lights everywhere, spinning round and round. Laura thought she was dying.
5. A sudden blackness that lasts a long time.
6. She wakes up and discovers that around an hour has passed which she cannot account for.

Medical tests were instigated in June 1984. Laura was also experiencing a twitching of the arms and legs, in the evening and early morning, sometimes with more violent movements of the right arm. After the first examination, the consultant wrote to her GP, saying, 'I could not find any neurological abnormality on examination. The attack she describes I think is a prolonged episode of nocturnal myoclonus.'

'Myoclonus' is a neurological illness which causes the muscles to spasm. A week later Laura had an electroencephalogram (EEG) which 'showed distinct abnormalities precipitated particularly by hyperventilation in the right posterior quadrant'. It was decided that these abnormalities were connected to Laura's twitching and she was put on an anticonvulsant drug called carbamazepine. The drug failed to have any effect, even when the daily dose was increased from 400 mg to 600 mg.

On 7 May 1985 Laura was admitted into hospital 'for more detailed neurological investigation' and her medication was changed to clonazepam. This, like carbamazepine, is a drug used to treat all forms of epilepsy. Again, the drug had no effect, and Laura was discharged one week later.

The registrar in neurology noted that Laura 'was a pleasant, well-orientated girl'. He referred to Laura's 'falling sensation' (sinking feeling), 'momentary loss of consciousness or a flash of light in front of her eyes'. An examination found that there were 'no focal neurological signs' to explain the phenomenon. The registrar concluded:

CT scan normal. EEG showed excessive background slow activity with a right-sided emphasis that would be consistent with poorly controlled epilepsy, but was however, rather non-specific.

Clinically it seems likely that this girl had temporal lobe fits with a recent history of bilateral myoclonus, and a right body focal fit.

It was decided to obtain a 24-hour EEG for Laura which took place on 10 May. Any doubts that she might be suffering from epilepsy were compounded by the report prepared by the registrar after the test:

The EEG record showed no electro-physiological abnormalities during the twenty-four hour period. She tells me she had her normal jerking movements during this, and it seems likely therefore that these episodes are not all due to epilepsy. I must say that this situation is fairly difficult to assess. I have told her that I expected a lot of the jerking would disappear by itself.

Nevertheless, Laura was kept on carbamazepine with the addition of another anti-epilepsy drug, valproate. Although she continued to experience the sinking feeling, the doctors still prescribed the drugs. When there were lulls in the attacks the neurologists assumed it was due to the medication. By April 1987 it was being suggested that some of the psychological effects were hypnagogic attacks.

During the brief period at the onset of sleep, some people can experience very vivid hallucinations, known as 'hypnagogic imagery'. When they occur on awakening, the hallucinations are known as 'hypnopompic imagery'. They are said to convey an overwhelming sense of reality.

In the autumn of 1987 Laura was once again discharged from hospital, none the wiser about what, if anything, was physiologically wrong with her. During ten years of investigation, Laura saw *eleven* different neurologists. She felt that the specialists treated her for epilepsy because they could not conceive of there being any other explanation. She had, however, told them only a tiny part of the story and they were not aware that her two sisters were also experiencing the sinking feeling and paralysis.

In February 1993, after our investigation had begun, Laura wrote to the British Epilepsy Association outlining her symptoms. Their reply added to the confusion:

My colleague, Mrs Stewart, has discussed the contents of your letter with Dr Beecher, a specialist in epilepsy. Dr Beecher feels that the symptoms you have been experiencing are not epilepsy, but may be a neurological condition known as 'sleep paralysis', which has genetic features.

What was this added complication?

Paralysed

As we have seen, all four women at Black Brook Farm experienced the sensation of paralysis coupled with a feeling that there was a presence in the room, sometimes in bed with them. This continues to be the case, even though the girls now live at different addresses. A high percentage of abductees describe this paralysis as part of their experience. Neurologists think they have the answer. They call it 'sleep paralysis'.

Sleep paralysis was reported by a surprising cross-section of Americans in a recent survey. At the Abduction Study Conference at MIT in Cambridge, Massachusetts, Dr David J. Hufford, a folklorist not primarily interested in abductions, presented material gleaned from studies of people who had reported awakening paralysed. He was able to link this information to reports from all over the world throughout history.

In studies of university students unconnected with UFO encounters, as many as 20 per cent of those surveyed reported the experience of waking up unable to move and either sensing a presence in the room or the feeling actual weight of 'the Old Hag' on their chest. Dr Hufford, startled by this figure, investigated further and was able to confirm that this experience is world-wide, the same details being reported by a wide variety of countries and cultures.

He was unable to obtain funding for a large, sophisticated study, but he conducted his own survey in the USA and found that in the general population, among people who had no prior knowledge of the phenomenon, as much as 17 per cent of those interviewed had experienced this inability to move on waking. The paralysis was usually almost total, the eyes being the exception.

There was also an amazing similarity of experience among the 17 per cent: over 75 per cent of them were on their backs when they woke up, just under 90 per cent of them felt threatened by a presence in the room, and just under 50 per cent of them felt a pressure on the chest.

Dr Hufford has a scientific explanation for this phenomenon which answers many of the questions, but leaves an important one unanswered. His study seems to show that awakening paralysed is related to REM sleep, a phase associated with dreaming. Hufford observes that in this stage of altered consciousness the body becomes extremely relaxed and muscles do not respond to the commands of the brain. This is thought to be a safety feature, to stop people who are dreaming about murdering their partners from carrying out the act in their sleep! He suggests that the sensations of paralysis occur when the subject wakes up from REM sleep and the relaxed state of the REM condition persists. The fact the eye muscles are not paralysed seems to reinforce Hufford's hypothesis. However, he is not suggesting that this is a complete explanation:

At present 'sleep paralysis' is not an explanation, even though some of its neurological mechanisms are known with reasonable confidence - rather that sleep paralysis itself is an anomaly on a par with abductions.

Dr Hufford is the first to point out that his theory does not account for the overwhelming similarity of his subjects' experiences. They seem to have the same sort of fears and physical sensations. Can it be that they are all awakening from similar dreams – nightmares of pursuit, fear, hauntings – and these dream feelings linger for a while in the paralysed, yet waking, state? Such interesting possibilities should be investigated further, as they have an obvious connection with the abductee phenomenon.

Ronald Siegel, an associate research professor in the UCLA School of Medicine's Department of Psychiatry and Behavioral Sciences, did not have to depend on the accounts of other people for details of the phenomenon, having fallen victim to it himself. In his book *Fire In The Brain* he describes being woken in the early hours by the sound of his bedroom door opening. He then saw a 'murky presence' and heard footsteps approaching the bed. As he tried to throw back the quilt, Siegel found he was pinned to the bed and felt a weight on his chest. As he strained to breathe he caught a whiff of a dry dusty odour. Then a shadow fell across the bedside clock, something touched his arm and neck and a female voice whispered in his ear. The words, although unintelligible, conjured up images of rotting swamps, toadstools and 'hideous reptiles'.

He tried to move once more but the pressure increased. A cold hand grasped his arms and something straddled him. The bed-springs began to creak. He *knew* the being was evil. As he began to lose consciousness, the voice stopped and he heard the intruder moving slowly out of the room. Gradually the pressure on his chest eased. He searched the house, but it was empty. The experience had lasted ten minutes.

Professor Siegel explains this very vivid and horrific experience in terms of sleep paralysis coupled with hypnopompic hallucinations. The tenth neurologist to evaluate Laura Bond reached the same conclusion in her case. In a letter to her GP dated May 1993, the ghost of TLE was finally laid to rest:

I do not think these attacks are epilepsy. I think she has predominantly sleep paralysis but also hypnagogic hallucinations. Sometimes in the state between sleep and awakening she sees things and hears things which are not there. Her sister has similar problems.

Siegel goes to great lengths to rationalize his experience, reducing it to a conjuring trick played on the conscious mind by the unconscious. It would be refreshing – and easier – to take it at face value and trust his original perceptions. An entity entered the room, paralysed him, then mounted him for its own gratification. This is not to suggest that the experience should be accepted without question, but it would make sense for a superior being to control its victim using paralysis.

Paralysis sometimes occurs before a supernatural event. Philip Spencer wanted to run away from the being on Ilkley Moor, but he was paralysed. Abductees find themselves unable to move when placed on a table ready for examination. 'Sleep paralysis' is a convenient label for medical experts to use to explain such anomalous experiences. The incident cannot be literally true, it has to have a rational explanation, even when that explanation relies on supposition and conjecture and does not fit all the facts. If a being could paralyse a person's muscles, the outward effects would be identical to those of sleep paralysis.

Laura purposely kept the full details of her experiences from her doctors for most of the time she was being tested. It was only in 1993 that she told them that one of her sisters had the same 'symptoms'. In January 1994 she took the very brave step of telling neurologist No. 11 the whole story: the UFO, the apparitions, the poltergeist activity, the out-of-body experience and the nocturnal intrusions into her house. She described how her two sisters had had similar experiences and their children were also being affected.

When Laura went to see him for the second time (the last time she would see any 'expert'), the neurologist barely looked up from his desk as she stood patiently waiting. Then he pushed a prescription for drugs across the polished surface and said, 'Try these and come back in two months.' Laura went home and threw the paper on the fire.

How can sleep paralysis be the answer when often the victims are not even asleep? In December 1992 Laura reported the following:

I awoke at 4.30 am as my oldest daughter was coughing badly. After going downstairs for some medicine, she climbed into bed with me. That's when it happened. I kept opening my eyes until the numbness fully took hold. It made me overwhelmingly tired and then I hit some blackness. I didn't wake up until 8 am.

Laura remembers a burning, tingling, sensation on her back and was left with a headache.

Peter Hough investigated the story of a haunted bypass at Stocksbridge, a small town north of Sheffield. It was a well-attested case with a number of reputable witnesses, including two police officers. Special Constable Beet and PC Ellis were parked up on the deserted and unfinished road one night in 1987, a week after two security men had fled in terror after seeing a hooded figure on the site. As they sat in their police car, a strange sensation came over Ellis:

Suddenly I had a feeling, unlike any I'd had before, just as if some-

one had walked over my grave, because I froze. And what was so odd, I went cold without knowing why. It was a feeling of total helplessness, like I was paralysed. I couldn't move my arms, I couldn't move my legs, I couldn't speak.

This was a prelude to the materialization of a strange figure at PC Ellis's side of the car – an apparition also witnessed by his colleague. As a blanket explanation for the paralysis that takes hold of experients at the onset of a paranormal event, so-called sleep paralysis leaves a lot to be desired.

Chapter 17

The Answer to Everything?

fter her hypnosis, Susan Bond suffered from nightmares in her London home. One morning as she began to wake up a feeling of exhilaration washed over her. A single thought pounded her head. *She knew the answer to everything*. At last it all made sense! But as she awoke fully the thought slipped away like a trickle of water down a storm drain.

Susan's mother, Joyce, also told us:

This has happened to me, too, although it was some time before the hypnosis. I woke up knowing I had the answer, and knew what it all meant, but immediately on waking it was gone. I don't even know what it was about, except it felt of great importance.

Jayne wrote and told us in December 1993:

The other night I woke up with a feeling of amazement and felt gloriously happy. I knew the answer – I knew what was going on! I also knew that I would forget it very quickly, so I woke up Andrew and told him I had something very important to say. A moment later Christopher had an asthma attack. I sorted him out and promptly forgot what I had just told my husband. I woke him up again and asked him what I had said, and he had forgotten too. This isn't the first time I've remembered something incredible, then immediately forgotten it again.

Philip Spencer said that the event on Ilkley Moor had made him more uncertain about things, more sceptical of the world. This, perhaps, is a natural consequence, but the women at Black Brook Farm believe that the phenomenon played an active and positive part in their lives. As Jayne explained, 'I think – in fact, we all believe this – that the UFO changed the way we think. It somehow altered our consciousness. We have become more aware, more caring.'

This happens to a lot of subjects. They become concerned about environmental issues, change their eating habits and think more deeply about things. They do not necessarily turn to religion or become New Agers; the changes are deep, but outwardly more subtle. It would be nice to believe that benevolent extraterrestrials are abducting humans to warn them about the dangers to humanity and altering them in some beneficial way. However, as we have seen, many of the reported experiences have been quite horrific. Some of those involved have suffered from post-traumatic stress.

Even with encounters that appear friendly, when the layers are stripped away to expose a fuller memory, a more sinister episode emerges. The smiling friendly entity that tried to lure Abigail away in her back garden turned nasty when the child's mother called her in. Samantha and Malcolm's apparently innocuous experience in France caused some of her hair to fall out, due, most likely, to stress associated with buried memories too terrible to face.

Many American accounts of abductions and close encounters describe procedures that remind us more of experiments carried out by Nazi scientists than kind, caring aliens. Janet, in Chapter 3, believes that the entities made physical adjustments to her body – with disastrous consequences. Yet the psychiatrists and therapists dealing with these people tell them what a positive experience they have had, how the extraterrestrials are wonderful and are, with their help, trying to save the world from impending doom. This is a prime example of George Orwell's 'double-think'. The abductees, after being humiliated and manipulated by creatures from a nightmare, hear their therapists tell them that the experience is 'character-building'.

In April 1995 we were fortunate to meet Professor Leo Sprinkle, who was leading a delegation of American abductees and therapists to Britain. Sprinkle is a veteran abduction researcher, a kind and amusing man for whom we have a lot of respect. However, we were very worried by what we heard during the discussion with his party of psychologists and abductees in a Manchester hotel.

As we talked it became apparent that the psychologists had also had experiences with extraterrestrials. Did this give them a deeper insight into the problems of their patients, or was it a case of the blind leading the blind? They saw their role as carers, helping their clients come to terms with their abduction by alien beings. What they were actually doing was reinforcing a belief which may prove to be completely erroneous.

A properly trained psychoanalyst does not enter into debate about or even discussion of the details his client brings to the analysis. He remains a non-judgemental listener, but does, however, insist that his patients say what they are thinking. If we consider the work of those who take the remembered or reported experiences of abductees at face value and seek to build a structure from them, we can see the folly of such a literal approach.

What, then, is the truth behind alien abductions? We have demonstrated beyond reasonable doubt that the aliens are one face of a dark crystal that has also spawned demons, fairies, apparitions, Men in Black and Bogus Social Workers. Dr Simon Taylor's conclusion that the beings who took him and his friend for a ride in a UFO were really the jinn is probably correct. But are the jinn just another skin of the onion?

The phenomenon *wants* us to believe it is extraterrestrial in origin. In fact, abductees and close-encounter subjects are presented with a piece of theatre in which they take a leading role. Who, or what, writes the scripts and why are particular plots and story lines chosen? We agree that there is a psychological component to the mystery, but is this component merely a prop used by an alien intelligence to further its agenda, or is it the *raison d'être* of the entire phenomenon?

At the end of five years of investigation, Moyshe Kalman has not seen or heard anything that lends credibility to a literal acceptance of the stories the percipients have told. Yet he believes that most of the story-tellers are sincere; and much of what they recall is inexplicable. He is sure that something highly unusual has happened in their lives, but that 'something' is a feature of human existence in all ages and at all times.

UFO encounters and abductions are *not* wish-fulfilment. Many percipients do not want to believe the literal interpretation of their experiences. Peter Hough vividly remembers one abductee who, after after a particularly traumatic session of hypnosis, stood with tears rolling down her cheeks, begging him and the psychologist present to tell her that what she had recalled was just a fantasy, make-believe, a dream. They could not oblige.

We have examined the psychological and neurological mechanisms which the sceptics claim account for abduction experiences. While not ruling them out altogether, we found them wanting as an overall and complete explanation. The reductionists need to explain, for instance:

1 The bleeding that many experients report immediately after an abduction.
2 Illnesses suffered in the aftermath of an experience.
3 The pressure which close-encounter subjects describe feeling on their head and shoulders.
4 The injuries which abductees receive, apparently as a consequence of an abduction.
5 Why percipients cannot wake their partners at the onset of an encounter.
6 The long periods of 'missing time'.
7 Multiple abductions.
8 The independent corroboration of UFO sightings in connection with abductions.

Various medical experts thought that Laura Bond was suffering from TLE and, until they changed their opinion, put her on drugs. Epilepsy was seen as the only explanation for her symptoms. If hers was a neurological condition, was it possible for her two sisters to share it, to the extent of suffering similar attacks at the same time?

Laura told us about a weekend when she and her husband went away in their caravan. The couple were sitting reading when Laura felt the sinking feeling taking hold. She was so used to it by then that she did not mention it to William. During her silent attack, he suddenly got up and went outside. The young man returned a few minutes later and said to his wife, somewhat sheepishly, 'You know that strange feeling you get? Just now when we were reading it came over me. I just had to get out.' *They had both had an attack, simultaneously.*

One day, without any knowledge of Laura's experiences, Pat, a neighbour, confided that she had been suffering from a strange tugging sensation, as if she was being pulled down into something.

The problem with attributing a wholly subjective cause to abductions is the apparently concrete nature of the peripheral phenomena. UFOs – whatever they turn out to be – are objectively real. The evidence is mounting day after day, year after year. We have little doubt that Samantha and Malcolm in France and the Bonds and their neighbours in Lincolnshire accurately described an object unlike any known aircraft in structure or performance.

What of the Ilkley case, where the percipient, a former police officer, produced what he claimed was a photograph of one of his alien abductors? We do not know whether the picture is genuine or not. Often, evidence of this kind has to be measured against the subject's character. Those who know Philip Spencer do not doubt his honesty. If you trust someone in every other respect, is it fair – or even rational – to doubt their integrity when they present you with something which does not fit the generally understood concept of reality? If not, Philip Spencer has provided proof of the physical existence of aliens. Something is playing conjuring tricks with our reality.

It is clear from their bizarre dress and behaviour that the MIB are an integral part of the phenomenon. They are not hallucinations brought about by epilepsy or hypnagogic states because they have often been seen by a number of witnesses and visit for minutes or even hours, not seconds. If we do not doubt the MIB, how can we deny the objective reality of extraterrestrials?

The problem is that the aliens are not alien enough. In appearance, they come straight out of 'sci-fi' comic books and they do exactly what unsophisticated science-fiction writers would predict: examine and experiment on human beings. In the 1960s and early 1970s, close-encounter witnesses described seeing aliens taking soil samples. That was what astronauts were doing on the moon at the time, so people expected visiting aliens to do the same on Earth. Samantha apparently saw some 'men' digging up her front garden, and maybe they were doing the same thing. Today, however, such a report is the exception rather than the rule. It all comes down to expectations.

Some critics say that UFOs should be left to the ufologists and abductees left to the psychiatrists. They believe that, while there is objective evidence for UFOs, the evidence for abduction by aliens is too anecdotal. Although we have some sympathy for that view, in reality, the two phenomena are too closely bound up with one another to be separated. *There has to be a causal relationship*.

After a UFO close encounter, many witnesses claim that they 'feel different'. The women at Black Brook Farm believe that the object they saw somehow changed their consciousness. Jayne had the impression that the UFO was pumping streams of words into their minds.

Consciousness is the key to all this. Bewilderingly, there also seems to be a physical aspect. Dr Taylor's flight in the UFO seems very dream-like. When the object swooped down so low that Simon thought he could reach out and touch some sheep, the animals apparently did not react in their normal manner and run away. Yet this was a shared experience: the two men lost six hours and then found themselves near the village instead of back on the mountain. Their abduction at Ahar was a prelude to several days of UFO activity and, in one case at least, there was undeniable proof of the physical reality of the alien craft.

There is some indication that abductions take place when the victim is in an out-of-body state. An American abductee, Linda Napolitano, was floated out of her apartment through a closed window and Janet remembers the aliens teaching her to pass through solid objects.

Are we wrong to answer one unknown with another? Certainly, there is no proof that people are physically abducted. Are abductees in an altered state of consciousness?

Although many of the experiences he describes are essentially dream-like, Whitley Strieber believes that alien beings can manifest in our reality too. In best fairy-tale tradition, one of the aliens he saw told him that their appearance was not their true form. When entering our world they 'wear' bodies, just as we would wear a diving-suit in order to explore the ocean bed.

The only concept which in any way suggests an explanation for abductions and associated phenomena is the idea that we are victim to intrusions from other dimensions. This theory was championed by the journalist/investigator John Keel and the computer scientist Dr Jacques Vallée.

Vallée draws attention to the work of modern physicists and their theories about a universe of many dimensions beyond the four that are familiar to us. The physicists Dr Michio Taku and Jennifer Trainer point out that in order for the theory of the Big Bang to work, five dimensions are required. Hugh Everett and John Wheeler of Princeton University, USA, proposed as far back as 1957 a 'Many Worlds Interpretation' of quantum mechanics in which the universe is viewed as constantly branching out into alternative realities.

Have intelligent life-forms in other realities found a way of breaching ours? UFOs, Vallée speculates, do not come from outer space, but from a 'multiverse' beyond space and time which is all around us. While accepting the physical manifestations of the phenomenon, Dr Vallée believes that:

These events take place in a reality we simply do not understand; they have an impact on a part of the human mind we have not discovered. I believe the UFO phenomenon is one of the ways through which an alien form of intelligence of incredible complexity is communicating with us symbolically.

What is the real meaning behind the encounters? When we try to teach nursery-school children about the complex world in which they are growing up, we tailor the lesson to their level of understanding and dress it up as play in order to retain their interest.

Is there an intelligence attempting to communicate with us? Does it gain access to our mental store of images and select what it believes are the appropriate ones to convey certain information? Are abductions and encounters with aliens metaphors for some deeper truth? If so, we have made the mistake of taking the imagery at face value without digging beneath the surface for the real meaning. Then again, the forces behind these phenomena could be so alien as to be completely beyond our comprehension – some percipients' experiences sound like a visit to a madhouse.

At the end of a lecture, Peter Hough is often asked, 'Why do they come here?' Hough sometimes replies, 'Perhaps we're just their entertainment.'

Bibliography

The following are a representative selection of sources used and consulted in the preparation of this book and are additional to the case studies discussed.

Barstow, A.L. *Witchcraze, A New History of the European Witch Hunts*, Pandora, 1994.

Bord, Janet and Colin *Sacred Waters*, Paladin, 1985.

Bowen, Charles (Editor) *The Humanoids*, Futura, 1977.

Boyd, Andrew *Blasphemous Rumours*, Fount, 1991.

Bryan, C.D.B. *Close Encounters Of The Fourth Kind*, Weidenfeld & Nicolson, 1995.

Budden, Albert *UFOs – Psychic Close Encounters: The Electromagnetic Indictment*, Blandford, 1995.

Ellenburger, Henri F. T*he Discovery of the Unconscious*, Basic Books, 1970.

Evans, Hilary and Spencer, John *UFOs 1947–1987*, Fortean Tomes,1987.

Friday, Ellen *Women On Top*, Arrow Books, 1991.

Fuller, John G. *The Interrupted Journey*, Souvenir Press, 1966.

Gauld, Alan *A History of Hypnotism*, Cambridge University Press,1992.

Gregory, Richard (Editor) *The Oxford Companion to The Mind*, Oxford University Press, 1987.

Hough, Peter and Randles, Jenny *The Complete Book of UFOs*, Piatkus, 1994.

Hough, Peter *Supernatural Britain*, Piatkus, 1995.

Hough, Peter *Witchcraft: A Strange Conflict*, The Lutterworth Press, 1991.

Jacobs, David M. *Secret Life*, Simon & Schuster, 1992.

Klass, Philip J. *UFO Abductions: A Dangerous Game*, Prometheus, 1989.

Lindner, Robert *The Fifty-Minute Hour*, Free Association Books, 1986.

Mack, John E. *Abduction*, Simon & Schuster, 1994.

Pazder, Lawrence *Michelle Remembers*, Sphere Books, 1980.

Pritchard, Andrea et al. *Alien Discussions*, North Cambridge Press, 1994.

Randles, Jenny *The Pennine UFO Mystery*, Grafton, 1983.

Randles, Jenny and Hough, Peter *Strange But True?*, Piatkus, 1994.

Renstak, Richard *The Brain*, Bantam Books, 1984.

Rosa, de Peter *Vicars of Christ, The Dark Side of the Papacy*, Corgi Books, 1988.

Strieber, Whitley *Communion*, Century, 1987.

Temple, Robert *Open to Suggestion*, Aquarian Press, 1989.

Terr, Lenore *Unchained Memories*, Basic Books, 1994.

Thornton, E.M. *Hypnotism, Hysteria and Epilepsy*, William Heinemann Medical Books, 1976.

Vallée, Jacques *Dimensions*, Souvenir, 1988.

Vallée, Jacques *Passport To Magonia*, Spearman, 1970.

Victor, Jeffrey S. *Satanic Panic*, Open Court, 1993.

Wentz, W.Y. Evans *The Fairy Faith in Celtic Countries*, Smythe, 1981.

Journals and magazines

Encounters, January 1996, 'Harry Harris, Investigator of UFOs'.

Nasr, Seyyed Hossein, 'The Jinn'.

Vogue, February 1996, Linda Grant, 'Are Women Mad?'

Index

A

Abigail 75-78, 80-84, 86-88, 130
Ahar 8, 16, 62
American Freedom of Information
    Act 12
Annecy 19
Atkins, Zoe 65-69

B

Barber, Theodore X 157
Basterfield, Keith 157
Beard, Carolyn 140
Beet, Special Constable 180
Bernheim, Dr 145
Birmingham 11
Black Brook Farm 91, 112, 118,
    119, 131, 138, 170, 187
Blackmore, Dr Sue 171
Bond, Jayne 91, 92, 94-99, 100-
    105, 108-111, 114, 116,118,
    121-123, 125, 126, 132, 182
Bond, Joyce 32, 91-94, 108, 114,
    119, 121, 127, 182
Bond, Laura 89, 91, 92, 93, 106,
    111-114, 117, 123,129, 130,
    131, 132, 137, 138, 142,
    172-176, 179, 180, 185
Bond, Susan 91, 93, 106, 114,
    119, 124, 182
Braid, Dr James 145
British Epilepsy Association 176
Brown, Bobby 138
Bruno, Joanne 155
Budden, Albert 169, 170
Bullard, Dr Eddie 62
Butterfield, William 55

C

Caignes Cordon 20, 23
Camilho, Jose 59

Carter, Mrs. 139
Chamran, Mustata 61, 62
Charcot, Jean Martin 145
Chaumont 22
Crawley, Geoffrey 42

D

Defense Intelligence Agency 12
Democritus 143
Devereux, Paul 168
Dijon 19, 22
Du Maurier, George 145
Dunn, Mark 139

E

East Morton 38
Eccles, Sir John 144
Elburz Mountains 14
Ellen, N. 164
Ellis, Police Constable 180
Epagny 19
Epilepsy 161-163
Erzerum 15
Esdale, Dr James 145
Evans Wentz, W.Y. 58
Everett, Hugh 188

F

False Memory Syndrome (FMS)
    149
Felix, Minucius 70
Finnegan, Matt 72
Foss, Detective Suprintendent 141
Frangy 20
Freud, Sigmund 108, 145
Freyd, Jennifer 150
Freyd, Peter 150
Friday, Dr Nancy 69
Friedrich, Karl 155

G
Gacy, John Wayne 85
Gilman, Paul 56
Gliedman, Dr John 172
Glover, Mark 88
Grant, Linda 149, 150
Griffiths, Frances 42
Grimsby 56

H
Harris, Dr Victor 72, 74
Hearst, Patty 68
Higgs, Dr Marietta 141
Hill, Barney 167
Hill, Betty 167
Hopkins, Budd 32, 115, 127
Hopkins, Dr Herbert 134, 135, 141
Hough, Peter 41, 42, 50, 51, 52, 55, 72, 99, 116, 120, 137, 139,180, 188
Hufford, Dr David J. 177, 178
Hughlings Jackson, Dr J. 161
Hynek, Prof. J. Allen 6

I
Ilkley Moor 44
Imam Reza 15
Imperial Iranian Air Force 12
Institoris, Heinrich 70
Isfahan 13

J
Jacobs, Dr David 32
Jacobson, Eric 155

K
Kalman, Moyshe 37, 65, 66, 68, 145, 156, 165
Keel, John 187
Kelly, Liz 44
Kermode, T. C. 58
Keul, Dr Alex 155
King, Stephen 85
Klass, Philip 172

Kramer, Heinrich 70

L
Lafreniere, Gyslaine 168
Lawson, Dr Alvin 153
Leonard, Prof. Raymond 43
Leucippus 143
Liverpool Albert Docks 27
London 11

M
Mack, Prof. John 152
Manchester 68, 139
Mantle, Philip 41
Marshall, Tony 41
Mashhad 13, 15
Massachusetts Institute of Technology 157, 177
McCall, Dr William 153
McCartney, Paul 168
MENSA 34
Mowlavi 17

N
Napolitano 113
Neurology, Institute of 169
New York 11
Nippon Television 42
NREM (Non-Rapid Eye Movement) 107

O
Osborne, Jack 94
Orwell, Geroge 183

P
Pal, Stephen 30, 130
Paris 11
Parnell, June 155
Pazder, Dr Lawrence 65
Penfield, Wilder 144
Pernambuco 59
Persinger, Michael 168, 171
Phillips, Ken 155
Popper, Sir Karl 144

Q

Qazuim 8
Qazvin 17
Qum 13

R

Radiological Protection Service 44
RAF Finningley 94
Randles, Jenny 41, 116
REM (Rapid Eye Movement) 178
Reynie, Nicholas de la 71
Reza 8, 15, 62
Riley, Sean 145-148
Ring, Prof. Kenneth 89
Roberts, Andy 41
Rochdale 68, 72
Rodeghier, Mark 158

S

Sacks, Mike 79
Satanic Ritual Abuse (SRA) 64
SAUAK 10
Shelley 100, 130, 135
Siegel, Ronald 178
Singleton, Jim 44, 49, 50, 52
Smith, Michelle 65
Spooner, Dr 43
Sprenger, Jakob 70
Sprinkle, Prof. Leo 155, 183
St Helens, Merseyside 85

Steech, Sandra 91, 92, 110
Stocksbridge 180
Strieber, Whitley 51, 60, 62, 108, 115, 172, 187
Sutcliffe, Albert 139
Sutcliffe, Peter 140
Sutherst, Peter 42

T

Taku, Dr Michio 188
Tall Ships Parade 31
Tate, Henry 51
Taylor, Dr Simon 8-18, 58, 59, 61, 184, 187
Tehran 8, 11, 12, 14, 17
Terr, Dr 150, 151
Thornton, E.M. 163
Tomlinson, Arthur 43
Trainer, Jennifer 188

V

Vallée, Dr Jacques 187
Ventura 30

W

Walker, Dr M.C. 169, 171
Wheeler, John 188
Wilson, Sheryl C. 157
Wright, Elsie 42
Wyatt, Dr Geoffrey 141